You Can Write for Children

How to Write
Great Stories, Articles, and Books
for Kids and Teenagers

by Chris Eboch

You Can Write for Children

How to Write
Great Stories, Articles, and Books
for Kids and Teenagers

by Chris Eboch

Pig River Press, Socorro, New Mexico

Contents

You Can Write for Children

Remember the magic of bedtime stories? When you write for children, you have the most appreciative audience in the world. But to reach that audience, you need to write fresh, dynamic stories, whether you're writing rhymed picture books, middle grade mysteries, edgy teen novels, nonfiction, or something else.

In this book, you will learn:

How to explore the wide variety of age ranges, genres, and styles in writing stories, articles, and books for young people.

How to find ideas.

How to develop an idea into a story, article, or book.

The basics of character development, plot, setting, and theme – and some advanced aspects.

How to use point of view, dialogue, and thoughts.

How to edit your work and get critiques.

Where to learn more on various subjects.

This book does not focus on the business side of writing. I won't be addressing query letters, submissions, editors, or agents. I'm not going to talk about marketing and publicity. This is about how to tell a good story. I'll point you toward resources to learn more, if you should choose to do so. But most people spend too much time worrying about selling their work, and not enough time focusing on writing well. Not only is that counterproductive, but it takes the fun out of writing.

This is an introduction to the *craft* of writing for children. It will help you get started, through straightforward information and exercises you can do on your own or with critique partners. If you've been writing for awhile but feel your writing education has gaps, this guide can help you work through those weak points. I share examples from my own work and teaching experience, along with interviews and advice from other published writers and industry professionals. (In the interviews, job titles were accurate when the interview was written, but may have changed since.)

Why We Write

Before we get into specifics, I want to talk briefly about goals. It is possible to make money writing for children. Some people even make a modest living from writing. Estimates say about 5% of published authors can support themselves through their writing. However, if you want to get rich quick, then writing – especially writing for children – is not the way to do it. You might as well play the lottery or try to get on one of those talent TV shows.

But there are other reasons to write. Perhaps you want to record family stories or write down some of the bedtime stories you told your children or grandchildren. Maybe you enjoy the creative expression of developing stories. Maybe you have ideas, thoughts, messages, or entire worlds to share. As my friend Jennifer says, "If I don't write down the voices in my head, people would just think I'm crazy."

The point is, *you* get to choose your goals. At times other people may try to push you one way or another. Writing classes may focus on query letters, networking, or marketing. Well-meaning friends and family may encourage you to self-publish or submit your work to publishers. Try to remember why you want to write, and focus on your own goals, whatever they are. Hopefully learning and having fun are part of those goals.

If you choose to write for publication, you can get there with patience and perseverance. You'll find many opportunities, some of which may come as a surprise. Most Kid Lit authors start out wanting to write either picture books or novels, but the market doesn't end there. Schools and libraries need nonfiction books for all ages. Magazines publish articles, short stories, poems, crafts, and activities. You may find it easier to break in with a magazine piece than with a book manuscript, and some authors find regular work in magazines. Learn more in Chapter 1, Market Research.

I will discuss some of the many different opportunities in writing for children – fiction and nonfiction, different genres and age ranges, books and magazines, etc. If you should eventually choose to submit your work for publication, you'll need to know all of that. But it's also useful for learning the craft of writing. You can explore new areas. You might discover you love something you didn't even know existed. And studying published works is a great way to learn to write well. Plus, it's fun!

Let's get started.

Chapter 1: Market Research

Writing for children covers a broad range of styles, topics, lengths, and age ranges. These include both fiction and nonfiction, in books, magazines, and more. Exploring will help you decide where you feel comfortable. If you want to write for publication, you'll need a good understanding of what's being published. Even if you are writing purely for your own enjoyment, or to share stories with your family, studying other children's literature will make you a better writer. It may also inspire new ideas!

Maybe you are already an avid reader of recent children's literature. If so, great! If not, it's time to start. You'll learn a lot and get to enjoy wonderful stories at the same time. The library is an excellent place to explore children's lit, but make sure you look for recent books or magazines. Styles have changed over the years, so it's best to focus on books published in the last five years.

Try keeping notes on what you read, if you don't already. Did you enjoy the book? Why or why not? What aspects did you think worked well, and what could have been stronger? The patterns you pick up will tell you something about the children's book industry, but they'll tell you even more about yourself. Maybe you are attracted to funny stories for younger kids. Or perhaps you love complex fantasy novels with fabulous world building. If you are going to write, why not write what you love to read?

If you want to write for publication, you can also start researching agents and publishers here. When you read books you love, or ones that seem similar to your work, make a note of the publisher. You may also be able to identify the author's agent in the acknowledgments, or from the author's website. This will help you learn which publishers are producing what type of books. When you have something appropriate to submit, you'll have a list of agents or publishers that are suitable. You can also mention in your query letter that you are submitting to that person because of the kind of work they handle, giving examples from your reading.

Think about how to organize your notes so they'll be useful in the future. Should you keep a reading notebook, set up a spreadsheet, or use color-coded index cards? Find a system that works for you.

Studying Magazines

If you are fairly new to modern children's lit, study **magazines** for a good overview. The Cricket Magazine Group is a great place to start. They publish 14 magazines. Some are fiction and some are nonfiction, and they cover age ranges from birth to teen. You can read an online sample of each magazine on their website: http://www.cricketmag.com/534-Online-Samples

You may have a good idea of what you want to write; for example, maybe you are primarily interested in fiction for ages 4-6. But give the other magazines a look anyway. You may have a great idea that would be better for a different age range.

Also, a lot of people are intimidated by nonfiction but then find writing articles fun and interesting once they try a few. As a bonus, it can be easier to sell nonfiction because there's more demand for nonfiction articles, but fewer people write them. Most children's magazines use some nonfiction but not get many submissions. For example, *Highlights* publishes about equal amounts of fiction and nonfiction, but I've heard the magazine receives about 90% fiction submissions. And then there are many magazines focused on topics such as science and history, which only publish nonfiction.

With some digging, you can find hundreds of other magazines targeted at children, or at parents or teachers. *Magazine Markets for Children's Writers* and *Children's Writers and Illustrators Market* have listings. (I find the former a little easier to use, but you're more likely to find the latter at your local library.) A search for "children's magazines" will also bring up lots of links. Many are sites selling magazines, but they give you an overview of what's being published. If you are interested in writing about a particular sport or hobby, you might find a children's magazine that addresses it. Most religious groups also have their own magazines for children.

Learn from Reading

Once you identify a couple of magazines that interest you, check out their writer's guidelines. An internet search for the magazine's name plus "writer's guidelines" or "submission guidelines" usually does the trick. It's important to study those guidelines, and also actual copies of the magazine, before you submit work. Even magazines that seem similar can be quite different in their requirements. For example, some religious magazines focus on Bible stories, while others want realistic modern fiction or true anecdotes. In some, the message can be subtle and God need not be mentioned, while in others, the focus should be on God providing guidance.

You might also get ideas for how best to craft an article or story that will appeal to that magazine's editor. Studying *National Geographic Kids* several years ago, I noticed that most articles were broken into short bites of information, such as "10 Cool Things about Dolphins." If I wanted to pitch an article to them, I'd try to do something similar.

Study the magazines and submission guidelines, making a note of the type of content and target audience. Here are some questions to ask:

- What is the target age level?
- Do they use both fiction and nonfiction? If so, what is the rough percentage of each?
- What is their maximum word count? Do most of the stories/articles seem to be at the longer end of the range or at the shorter end?
- Are they open to submissions? What do they want (e.g., a query letter, a proposal, the complete manuscript, a writing sample)?
- Do they list any topics or genres they *don't* want? (e.g., no talking animals, true stories only, etc.) Note that some magazines may use their own staff for certain items. For example, they may publish puzzles, but do them all "in house" so they don't take submissions of puzzles.

See Chapter 19: Writing Magazine Nonfiction, for more advice on the magazine market.

Book Markets

Are you more interested in **picture books**? There are important differences between a picture book and a short story, so you need to know which you are really writing and all the elements a picture book needs! (Learn more in Chapter 18: Picture Book Versus Short Story.)

To prepare to write a picture book, you might review several of your favorite books, or see what's new at the library or bookstore. It wouldn't hurt to check out some of those magazines as well. They're still a good source for understanding the interests and reading abilities of children at different ages. Plus, you might try comparing some magazine stories and some picture books to see if you can identify the differences.

You'll find more on picture books later in this book. Briefly, picture books are usually under 1000 words, often under 500 words. They should have at least 12 different scenes that can be illustrated.

Nonfiction picture books and some folktales and fairytales can be longer, up to 2500 words or so, but it's harder to find a market for these. Look for similar books at the library or bookstore and see who publishes them.

Easy Reader books are designed to help kids learn to read. They use simple vocabularies and short sentences, appropriate to a particular reading level. They may be a few hundred words long or several thousand words, depending on the reading level. Often they have a few illustrations, maybe one per chapter. Some publishers specialize in this kind of work, while others do not produce these books at all. They may also be called early readers, early chapter books, beginning readers, and so forth. For more on this kind of book, see *Yes! You Can Learn How to Write Beginning Readers and Chapter Books*, by Nancy Sanders.

If you want to write **novels**, maybe you already have ideas, a work in progress, or finished manuscripts. If you feel comfortable with your understanding of the children's book market, and you already have a project in the works, you can skip this market overview.

If you are less confident, you might review some recent children's novels you've read and try to identify what made them successful or not successful for you. Reviewing magazines for middle grade and young adult readers can also be a way to tune into the differences between these groups – an important step in knowing what you are writing.

You'll find a lot of variety in novel lengths. Most middle grade novels (for ages 8 or 9 to 12) run between 25,000 and 50,000 words. Depending on how the pages are laid out, that can be 100 to 300 pages. Fantasy novels may be longer. Young adult novels, for teenagers, can fall within that same word count range, or they can be longer.

Regardless of length, novels should be packed full of action and character development. Young people don't have much patience for long-winded, boring material. Most novelists find they have to do a lot of revising to cut out the boring parts, add more excitement, and tighten the writing so it reads quickly and smoothly. Expect to do several drafts of a novel. Many professional writers say they do 10 to 20 drafts or more.

Market listings:

Children's Writer's & Illustrator's Market
Magazine Markets for Children's Writers
Book Markets for Children's Writers
The Society of Children's Book Writers and Illustrators (SCBWI) provides members with *THE BOOK*, which includes market surveys and directories for agents. The quarterly SCBWI *Bulletin* provides market updates.

A Note on Genre

Works of literature can be categorized by genre, although the categories are not clearly defined and distinct. Here are some possible genres:

Realistic Fiction
Humorous Fiction
Historical Fiction
Mystery, Thriller, or Suspense
Action and Adventure
Fantasy
Science Fiction
Horror
Nonfiction
Creative Nonfiction
Poetry

Many of these genres can be subdivided. For example, nonfiction includes biographies, history, science, and much more. Fantasy includes stories set in our modern world but using magical elements (the Harry Potter series); "high fantasy" set in a fictional world, often with characters such as wizards and goblins (*The Hobbit*); historical fantasy set in a realistic past time; time travel; and legends, fables, and fairy tales. Some people would include stories about ghosts, mind reading, or other supernatural talents/events within fantasy, while others would call paranormal a separate category.

Technically, "picture book" refers to the format rather than the genre. A picture book could also fit into one of the genres above.

Your local library or bookstore may have special shelves for adult mystery, romance, science fiction, and fantasy. This helps fans of a particular genre find books that suit them. Other fiction may be grouped together on the general fiction shelves. This could include everything from "literary" novels (often more serious, realistic novels with a focus on dramatic language) to smaller genres that don't get dedicated shelf space (historical fiction, humor, adventure) to mainstream genre titles. Some libraries may only separate out the paperback genre fiction, while hardcover titles are all shelved together by author name.

Books for children and teenagers are not as often separated by genre, as kids tend to read across genres. Some children's bookstores, or bookstores with large children's sections, will separate out teen books in certain genres, such as fantasy. However, most libraries and bookstores shelve children's fiction by target age range, sometimes with hardcover and paperback separated. In other words, you'll find the picture books together, the "learn to read" books together, and the middle grade novels together. Books for teenagers may be in a separate area. Nonfiction often has its own shelves.

Books do not necessarily have to fit into a clear genre. They may cross genres, as in a novel that combines mystery, fantasy, and romance. Genre categories should not be seen as a restriction. Still, it can be helpful to identify the genre of what you are writing. You may need this at several points in the writing and publishing process:

• When you are reading other books, so you can get a good feel for books in the genre you want to write. If you want to write fantasy, it helps to know what's been done and what kids love.

• When you're planning your book, so you can make sure it fits the appropriate genre. Will your book establish its genre quickly and stick to it throughout?

• When you're writing and editing your book, so you can make sure you stay on track. For example, if your goal is to write humor, is the book humorous throughout? If you are writing a mystery, is that the primary plot, with a strong climax and the mystery solved at the end?

- When you are researching and querying agents or editors. Make sure you are sending to people who like that genre, and let them know what genre your book is.
- When you are publishing and marketing your book. If you are self-publishing, you'll need to write the book description in a way that will attract the right readers. Regardless of how you publish, you'll want to share information on your website, on social media, and in person. Telling people "This is a picture book biography for early elementary" or "This is a humorous middle grade mystery" helps them grasp the idea immediately.

Chapter 2: Finding Ideas

Ideas are everywhere, including in our own lives. Of course, even the most exciting events may lack important story qualities such as character growth and strong plots. (We'll cover those qualities in upcoming chapters.) Still, personal and family experiences can provide the raw material to be molded into publishable stories and articles.

Amy Houts wrote *Down on the Farm*, about a girl on a farm vacation who wants to ride a horse but must do chores first. Houts was inspired by her own experiences, though not by a specific episode. "I was one of those horse-crazy girls," she says. "I knew how a girl could long to ride a horse."

Sometimes the smallest nugget can inspire a story. Susan Uhlig says, "My teen daughters and friends went on a mission trip to do a building project. The man overseeing the project was disappointed that there were no boys. I played the writer game of 'what if?' What if the man wouldn't let the team stay because they were all girls? That developed into a short story very easily — what he would say, my main character girl would do, how the problem would be solved, etc." The story sold to *Brio*.

Personally, I sold a story to *Highlights* based on the experience of finding frogs all over my neighborhood after a rainstorm. They also bought a historical story about the Mayan ballgame. That story, and my Mayan historical novel *The Well of Sacrifice*, were inspired by visiting Mayan ruins in Mexico and Central America.

Realistic, Not Real

Sometimes real life translates well into fiction — though a twist may make it more fun for children. Leslie Helakoski says, "My picture book, *Big Chickens*, is about all the things I was afraid of when young and I'd go into the woods with my brothers and sisters. I just turned us all into chickens and played with the language."

Caroline Hatton drew on school and home memories of growing up in Paris for her middle-grade novel, *Véro and Philippe*. Yet she did not simply write a memoir. "I wanted to write about a pet snail because I kept one in a shoebox in my family's apartment in Paris. But in my real life, my big brother left me and my pet snail alone – not much of a story, is it? So in the book, I made the brother threaten to eat the snail, as escargot."

Characters and outcomes may also change, Hatton points out. "My brother rigged a thing to scare me in the middle of the night. But in the book, I swapped roles, and it's the little sister who does it to her big brother. Sharing this with kids makes them howl with the pleasure of revenge."

Houts adds, "Most of the time I have to twist the reality of an experience so my story can include all the elements of good storytelling: a contrast of characters; a goal the main character strongly desires to reach; and believable obstacles the main character needs to overcome to reach her goal. Time needs to be cut down to a day or two. That condenses the action and makes the story more focused."

Author Renee Heiss says, "Use your life story as the skeleton, and then flesh it out with period details, colorful dialogue, and tons of sensory imagery to place your young readers into the time period and setting. It's not enough to tell what happened; you must show your readers your story and immerse them into your life as if they were a sibling growing up with you."

Asking friends and family members to share stories can provide ideas, while allowing you to turn the story into your own creation. Uhlig didn't witness the mission trip firsthand. "That freed me up to create problem, action, dialogue, etc. without being stuck on what really happened," she says.

You can "borrow" stories from history and the news as well. I found an interesting tidbit in a history of Washington State. A teenage boy had met bank robbers in the woods, and for some reason he told nobody about them. Why? This question, and my imagined answers to it, became my YA survival suspense *Bandits Peak*.

A Variety of Gems

Even if a specific episode doesn't make for a good story, the emotions you experience can give power to fiction. *Highlights for Children* Senior Editor Joëlle Dujardin says, "Past events that stick with you are probably memorable in large part due to your emotional response to them. Try to capture some of this feeling in your story without tying yourself to the events as they actually happened. For example, you might use your feelings about working with a difficult colleague to imagine being paired with a difficult classmate for a science project. Conveying genuine emotions will make your story feel richer."

Houts shares an example from *Down on the Farm*. "Because I had experienced the setting (a farm) and the action (chores/riding) I could write authentically. But there was something else about Emily's character that came directly from me and that was impatience. Impatience worked well in this story because Emily's goal isn't reached until close to the end when they finally get to ride."

"Drawing on real life is a great way to create believable settings, characters, and emotions in fiction," Dujardin adds. "Using unusual details from memory – the scent of Grandma's house, a particular pattern of wallpaper, the emotions related to standing up for a friend – can be a powerful way to give a story a feeling of authenticity."

Uhlig advises, "What happened to you is background material. You can use the setting and specific details, but the resulting story will not be a record of your experience. Instead, think about what you'd like readers to get out of a similar story. Focus on creating a problem and solution that shows that."

By mining real-life experiences, authors can find many gems of setting, character, plot, theme, or emotion that make for powerful fiction or nonfiction.

Beyond Research: Real-Life Nonfiction

If you want to write nonfiction, it makes sense to start by finding a topic that interests you, and which will hopefully interest young people as well. You'll want to do extensive research with reliable sources. But research alone is not always enough. Nonfiction comes to life when the writer steps away from the books. *Nature Friend* Editor Kevin Shank says, "It's easy to get an article based on research. We're short on stories where people went out and interacted with nature in a fun story. You can scribble notes when you're out in the field, and develop it when you come back home."

Personal and family events also make for strong nonfiction when they intersect with history. Pamela Tuck studied books from publisher Lee & Low. "They featured many courageous characters who weren't afraid to face down challenges. I felt that my dad's journey as a teenager participating in the Civil Rights Movement would be the perfect story." In the 1960s, her father won a local typing tournament, but because he was African-American, he didn't even receive an award. This became *As Fast As Words Could Fly*.

Louise May, Lee & Low Books Vice President/Editorial Director, notes, "This is a fascinating, very personal, civil rights story, one that highlights the courageous yet largely unknown actions that millions of people were taking every day just by living their lives with dignity as they fought for equality. You're not going to find a story like this in textbooks. Stories based on real-life experiences give readers a window into the experiences of everyday people, and can show how ordinary people rise to meet challenges. Readers can see something in the story that reflects their own lives or experiences. That's very empowering."

Adventures with travel or living abroad can also inspire stories. May says, "How exciting to learn about a new place through the eyes of someone who has been there! Authors who write based on their memories of traveling to different parts of the world have wonderful stories to tell, often filled with thrills, mishaps, discoveries, and lots of fascinating information."

Find the Arc

However, don't simply recite a list of facts. "There has to be a narrative arc – a beginning, middle, and end," May warns. "The manuscript cannot just be a vehicle for imparting information as a list of facts or experiences, to teach a lesson, or to deliver a message. It's important first to think about your audience – its age, overall prior knowledge, and interests – and then to choose your content accordingly. Consider why your experience would be interesting to others. Does it touch on a significant time in history? Does it include information or events that others may not know? Are the characters relatable? Is the outcome satisfying? Is it just plain fun?"

"A real-life event rarely follows a tight and satisfying story arc," says Dujardin from *Highlights*. "Selecting moments or details to give the story genuine flavor is great, but stick to the facts only when they're relevant and make for the most interesting plot." An author's first duty is to create a good story.

When writing nonfiction, you have to be truthful and accurate, but even nonfiction requires skillful editing of real-life events. Tuck says, "The most important thing is to choose one aspect as your focal point to build around. Then create a beginning that would lead up to that focal point, a middle that would show some type of conflict with it, and an ending that would show the results of your experience."

Make It Universal

Finally, to appeal to a wide audience, a story needs universal emotions and themes. Renee Heiss wrote *Woody's World* based on her parents, who lost everything during the stock market crash. She says, "The story I wrote was meant to show young readers that despite hardship, it is possible to come out of those problems with a positive attitude."

Kevin L. Lewis, Executive Editor at Disney-Hyperion Books, acquired a book by Matthew Cordell called *Wish*. Cordell and his wife had struggled with infertility issues, and he wanted to write a story that shared that experience with the children who resulted from such situations.

"Matt and I went back and forth with the project, trying to figure out how to serve Matt's original theme, while making a book anyone could appreciate," Lewis says. *Wish* now works, because "Matt had taken his personal struggle and his path to overcoming that struggle, and he had distilled a universal truth – that there is a willingness to endure, outlast, and overcome any obstacles in pursuit of a dream."

Lewis offers two pieces of advice. "First, it isn't always the happiest personal moments that lead to the most enriching stories. And second, taking the time to consider the similar (or parallel) experiences of those around you is a great step in reaching a larger audience. *Wish* began as the deeply personal story of individuals overcoming adversity. But it was only after acknowledging that there was a larger community of adversity with a broader range of stories to tell that the project could embrace a wider range of triumphs."

Finding the Seeds of Stories

Perhaps you picked up this book because you already have ideas. But maybe you're not sure what you want to write, or you have so many ideas you don't know where to start. Here are some options for brainstorming ideas. Take some time to relax and think about each question. Delve deep into your memories. Take lots of notes, even if you're not sure yet whether you want to pursue an idea. You can put each idea on a separate index card, or fill a notebook, or start a file folder with scraps of paper. Do whatever works for you.

Find story and article ideas based on your childhood experiences, fears, dreams, etc.:

• What's the scariest thing that happened to you as a child? The most exciting? The funniest?
• What's the most fun you ever had as a child? What were your favorite activities?
• What was the hardest thing you had to do as a child?
• What interested you as a child?
• When you were a child, what did you wish would happen?

Find story and article ideas based on the experiences of your children, grandchildren, students, or other young people you know:

• What interests them?
• What frightens them?
• What do they enjoy?
• What challenges do they face?
• What do their lives involve – school, sports, family, religion, clubs?

Other questions to consider:

What hobbies or interests do you have that might interest children?

What jobs or experiences have you had that could be a good starting point for an article or story?

Do you know about other cultures, or a particular time period?

What genres do you like? Would it be fun to write in that genre?

What genres did you like as a child? Did you love mysteries, ghost stories, fantasies, or science fiction? What were your favorite books? Why?

Look for inspiration in other stories, books, or TV shows. Can you take the premise and write a completely different story? Do you want to write something similar (a clever mystery, a holiday story, or whatever)? Do you want to retell a folktale or fable as a modern version, or with a cultural twist?

What do you see in the news? Is there a timely topic that could make a good article? If you read about kids doing something special, could you turn it into a profile for a children's magazine?

How might that news story work as fiction? Could you base a short story or novel on a true story about someone surviving danger or overcoming great odds?

Even the phonebook can provide inspiration. Check the Yellow Pages: Could you interview an automotive painter, animal trainer, or architect for an article? What would life be like for a child to have parents in that field? How about a teenager who dreams of entering the profession?

Wherever you look for ideas, search for things that are scary, exciting or funny – strong emotion makes a strong story.

Don't preach. Kids don't want to read about children learning lessons. All stories have themes, but when someone asks you about a mystery you read, you're probably not going to say, "It was a story about how crime doesn't pay." Rather, you'll talk about the exciting plot, the fascinating characters, perhaps even the unusual setting. A story's message should be subtle.

Getting started

Brainstorm 5 to 10 possible ideas for stories, articles, or novels for young people. Consider each one in turn. What would make the best place to start?

1. Focus your idea – be specific and narrow, especially with short stories or articles. Focus on an individual person and situation, not a universal ideal.

2. Ask yourself: What am I trying to accomplish?
Who am I trying to reach?
Why am I writing this?

3. Know your audience – study the genre and age range. If you're writing for publication, look up and follow publisher guidelines.

4. What do you need? Will you have to do research or conduct interviews?

With these notes, review your list of ideas and choose your top three. If you're writing for publication, identify three possible markets for each. If you can't find three possible markets, maybe it's not worth putting time into that idea. However, if you are writing purely for your own pleasure, for your family, or to develop your skills without thought of publication, skip this step – you can write whatever you want!

Chapter 3: Developing an Idea

Once you have your idea, it's time to develop it into an article, short story, or longer project. Of course, you can simply start writing and see what happens. Sometimes that's the best way to explore an idea and see which you want to say about it. But you might save time – and frustration – by thinking about the story in advance. You don't have to develop a formal, detailed outline, but a few ideas about what you want to say, and where you want the story to go, can help give you direction.

You can look at story structure in several ways. Here's one example of the parts of a story or article:

- A catchy **title**. The best titles hint at the genre or subject matter.

- A dramatic **beginning**, with a hook. A good beginning:
  – grabs the reader's attention with action, dialogue, or a hint of drama to come
  – sets the scene
  – indicates the genre and tone (in fiction) or the article type (in nonfiction)
  – has an appealing style

- A solid **middle**, which moves the story forward or fulfills the goal of the article.
  Fiction should focus on a plot that builds to a climax, with character development. Ideally the character changes by learning the lesson of the story.
  An article should focus on information directly related to the main topic. It should be organized in a logical way, with transitions between subtopics. The tone should be friendly and lively, not lecturing. Unfamiliar words should be defined within the text, or in a sidebar.

- A satisfying **ending** that wraps up the story or closes the article. Endings may circle back to the beginning, repeating an idea or scene, but showing change. The message should be clear here, but not preachy. What did the character learn?

- **Bonus material**: An article, short story, or picture book may use sidebars, crafts, recipes, photos, etc. to provide more value. For nonfiction, include a bibliography with several reliable sources. Novels do not typically have these things, but they may contain an author's note, a glossary of unfamiliar words, maps, or whatever makes the material more accessible and appealing. Classroom resources can be made available separately. For example, teachers can download lesson plans for use with my historical novels, *The Eyes of Pharaoh* and *The Well of Sacrifice*, on my website.

Developing an Idea

If you have a "great idea," but can't seem to go anywhere with it, you probably have a premise rather than a complete story plan. A story should have three parts: beginning, middle, and end (plus title and possibly bonus material). This can be a bit confusing though. Doesn't every story have a beginning, middle, and end? It has to start somewhere and end at some point, and other stuff is in the middle. Beginning, middle, and end!

Technically, yes, but certain things should happen at those points.

1. The beginning introduces a character with a problem or a goal.
2. During the middle of the story, that character tries to solve the problem or reach the goal. He probably fails a few times and has to try something else. Or he may make progress through several steps along the way. He should not solve the problem on the first try, however.
3. At the end, the main character solves the problem himself or reaches his goal through his own efforts.

You may find exceptions to these standard story rules, but it's best to stick with the basics until you know and understand them. They are standard because they work!

Teachers working with beginning writers often see stories with no conflict – no problem or goal. The story is more of a "slice of life." Things may happen, possibly even sweet or funny things, but the story does not seem to have a clear beginning, middle, and end; it lacks structure. Without conflict, the story is not that interesting.

You can have two basic types of conflict. An **external** conflict is something in the physical world. It could be a problem with another person, such as a bully at school, an annoying sibling, a criminal, or a fantastical being such as a troll or demon. External conflict would also include problems such as needing to travel a long distance in bad weather.

The other type of conflict is **internal**. This could be anything from fear of the dark to selfishness. It's a problem within the main character that she has to overcome or come to terms with.

An internal conflict is often expressed in an external way. If a child is afraid of the dark, we need to see that fear in action. If she's selfish, we need to see how selfishness is causing her problems. Note that the problems need to affect the child, not simply the adults around her. If a parent is annoyed or frustrated by a child's behavior, that's the parent's problem, not the child's. The child's goal may be the opposite of the parent's; the child may want to stay the same, while the parent wants the child to change.

For stories with internal conflict, the main character may or may not solve the external problem. The child who is afraid of the dark might get over that fear, or she might learn to live with it by keeping a flashlight by her bed. The child who is selfish and doesn't want to share his toys might fail to achieve that goal. Instead, he might learn the benefits of sharing.

However the problem is resolved, remember that the child main character should drive the solution. No adults stepping in to solve the problem! In the case where a child and a parent have different goals, it won't be satisfying to young readers if the parent "wins" by punishing the child. The child must see the benefit of changing and make a decision to do so.

A Story in Four Parts

If "beginning, middle, and end" doesn't really help you, here's another way to think of story structure. A story has four main parts: **situation, complications, climax,** and **resolution**. You need all of them to make your story work. (This is really the same as beginning, middle, and end, with the end broken into two parts, but the terms may be clearer.)

The **situation** should involve an interesting main character with a challenging problem or goal.

Even this takes development. Maybe you have a great challenge, but aren't sure why a character would have that goal. Or maybe your situation is interesting, but it doesn't actually involve a problem.

For example, I wanted to write about a brother and sister who travel with a ghost hunter TV show. The girl can see ghosts, but the boy can't. That gave me the characters and situation, but no problem or goal. Goals come from need or desire. What did they want that could sustain a series?

Tania feels sorry for the ghosts and wants to help them, while keeping her gift a secret from everyone but her brother. Jon wants to help and protect his sister, but sometimes he feels overwhelmed by the responsibility. Now we have characters with problems and goals. The story is off to a good start. (This became the four-book *Haunted* series.)

Tips:

• Make sure your idea is specific and narrow. Focus on an individual person and situation, not a universal concept. For example, don't try to write about "racism." Instead, write about one character facing racism in a particular situation.

• The longer the story, the higher the stakes needed to sustain it. A short story character might want to win a contest; a novel character might need to save the world.

• Ask why the goal is important to the character. Why does this particular individual desperately want to succeed in this challenge?

• Ask why this goal is difficult. If reaching the goal is too easy, there is little tension and the story is too short. The goal should be possible, but just barely. It might even seem impossible. The reader should believe that the main character could fail. (More on this in Chapter 5: Characters.)

• Even if your main problem is external, try giving the character an internal flaw that contributes to the difficulty. This adds complications and also makes your character seem more real. For some internal flaws, see the seven deadly sins: lust, gluttony, greed, sloth, wrath, envy, and pride.

• Test the idea. Change the character's age, gender, or looks. Change the point of view, setting, external conflict, or internal conflict. Choose the combination that has the most dramatic potential.

Building the Middle

If a character solves his goal easily, the story is boring. To keep tension high, you need **complications**.

For short stories, try the "rule of three" and have the main character try to solve the problem three times in different ways. The first two times, he fails and the situation worsens. **Remember: the situation should worsen.** If things stay the same, he still has a problem, but the tension is flat. If his first attempts make things worse, tension rises.

For novels, you may have even more attempts and failures. In my first Haunted book, *The Ghost on the Stairs*, I made sure each ghost encounter felt more dangerous. As Tania tries to get closer to the ghost in order to help her, Jon worries that she will go too far and be injured or even killed. With enough variety, you can sustain this kind of tension indefinitely (witness the ongoing battle between Harry and Voldemort in the seven-book Harry Potter series).

You can worsen the situation in several ways. The main character's actions could make the challenge more difficult. In my children's mystery set in ancient Egypt, *The Eyes of Pharaoh*, a young temple dancer searches for her missing friend. But when she asks questions at the barracks where he was a soldier, she attracts dangerous attention from his enemies.

The villain may also raise the stakes. In my Mayan historical drama, *The Well of Sacrifice*, the main character escapes a power-hungry high priest. He threatens to kill her entire family, forcing her to return to captivity.

Secondary characters can cause complications too, even if they are not "bad guys." In *The Ghost on the Stairs*, the kids' mother decides to spend the day with them, forcing them to come up with creative ways to investigate the ghost while under her watchful eyes.

Finally, the main character may simply run out of time. At her first attempt, she had a week. At her second attempt, she had a day. Those two attempts have failed, and now she has only an hour! That creates tension.

Tip:

• For each turning point in the story, brainstorm 10 things that could happen next. Then pick the one that is the worst or most unexpected, so long as it is still believable for the story.

Can She Do It?!

Your character has faced complications through the middle of the story. Finally, at the **climax**, the main character must succeed or fail. Time is running out. The race is near the end. The girl is about to date another guy. The villain is starting the battle. One way or another, your complications have set up a situation where it's now or never. However you get there, the climax will be strongest if it is truly the last chance. You lose tension if the reader believes the main character could fail this time, and simply try again tomorrow.

Tips:

• Don't rush the climax. Take the time to write the scene out in vivid detail, even if the action is happening fast. Think of how movies switch to slow motion, or use multiple shots of the same explosion, in order to give maximum impact to the climax. Use plenty of dramatic detail and your main character's thoughts and feelings to pull every bit of emotion out of the scene.

• To make the climax feel fast-paced, use mainly short sentences and short paragraphs. The reader's eyes move more quickly down the page, giving a sense of breathless speed. (This is a useful technique for cliffhanger chapter endings as well.)

Happy Endings

The climax ends with the **resolution**. You could say that the resolution finishes the climax, but it comes from the situation: it's how the main character finally meets that original challenge.

In almost all cases the main character should resolve the situation himself. No cavalry to the rescue! We've been rooting for the main character to succeed, so if someone else steals the climax away from him or her, it robs the story of tension and feels unfair.

Here's where many beginning children's writers fail. It's tempting to have an adult – a parent, grandparent, or teacher, or even a fairy, ghost, or other supernatural creature – step in to save the child or tell him what to do. But kids are inspired by reading about other children who tackle and resolve problems. It helps them believe they can meet their challenges, too. When adults take over, it shows kids as powerless and dependent on grownups.

Dianne K. Salerni, author of *The Eighth Day* series, says, "To be a writer of children's books, you need to be a child inside. You need to write like a child would write (except with the skill of an adult), and you need to read what your child-self wants to read. ... The best children's literature is written by adults who think they are still children, not by adults who want to 'help' children grow up."

Regardless of your character's age, let your main character control the story all the way to the end (though others may assist). For example, Sam Bond's *Cousins in Action* series is an ensemble featuring five cousins who have international adventures. The children take turns at being the hero throughout each book. In *Operation Golden Llama*, three of the young protagonists find themselves kidnapped on a mountainside in Peru. Their eleven-year-old cousin outwits the adults and treks through the jungle to come to their rescue. That may not be entirely realistic in real life, but it's great entertainment for young readers!

Although your main character should be responsible for the resolution, she doesn't necessarily have to succeed. She might, instead, realize that her goals have changed. The happy ending then comes from her new understanding of her real needs and wants. Some stories may even have an unhappy ending, where the main character's failure acts as a warning to readers. This is more common in literary novels than in genre fiction.

Tip:

- How the main character resolves the situation – whether she succeeds or fails, and what rewards or punishments she receives – will determine the theme. For example, a story with the theme "Love conquers all" would have a different resolution than a story with the theme "Love cannot always survive great hardship." Learn more about Theme in Chapter 13.

The next time you have a great idea but can't figure out what to do with it, check if you have all four parts of the story. If not, see if you can develop that idea into a complete, dramatic story or novel by expanding your idea, complications, climax, or resolution, as needed. Then readers will be asking you, "Where did you get that fabulous idea?"

Chapter 4: Point of View

Viewpoint is complex, and you can find entire books on the subject, but this overview should get you started. First of all, your point of view (POV) can be first-person, second-person, or third-person.

With **first-person** viewpoint, the main character is a narrator describing their actions using "I."
Here's an example from *The Well of Sacrifice*:

As soon as I had relaxed, I caught something out of the corner of my eye and froze again. A shadow behind me had moved.... By the time I got to the plaza, I could feel my heart pounding in my chest. I had seen no living thing, but a dozen demons seemed to threaten me.

Second-person viewpoint addresses the reader as "you." It is uncommon, but it does have uses in children's literature. "Choose Your Own Adventure" books ask the reader to make choices about where the story goes. An example might be something like this:

You enter a hallway and see one door to the left and one to the right. Which door do you choose?

In magazines, recipes and crafts typically address the reader, giving instructions. Some picture books talk directly to the reader, perhaps asking the child to take an action. For example, *Can You Make a Scary Face?* by Jan Thomas asks the reader to make faces.

Third-person viewpoint refers to the main character as she or he. Here's an example from my middle grade fantasy, *The Genie's Gift*:

Anise knew the candy must be enchanted. The genie cook always put some kind of protection on the food, so no one could eat it until he said so. Would it stick her jaws together so she couldn't speak? Turn her lips and tongue blue? Taste like camel dung? But Anise didn't want to wait until after the wedding. She was hungry now.

This is an example of third-person limited, where the viewpoint is close to a single person. Third-person POV can be omniscient, with an all-knowing outside narrator. More on that in a bit.

Viewpoint for Age

First-person viewpoint is a popular choice in young adult novels. Many people feel it helps the reader identify with the narrator. However, first-person viewpoint does not work well for young children. If a parent reads a picture book aloud, saying, "I did this, I did that," young children can get confused. They may not understand that the adult is speaking in the voice of a child character.

In general, it's best to use the third-person voice for picture books. Middle grade and YA novels can go either way. Sometimes a certain voice will "come to you," but you might want to experiment with different viewpoints. Some books work better with a little more distance between the main character and the reader. Others succeed by having a narrator who talks to the reader like a friend.

A trend in recent years is to use present tense in young adult novels. This makes it sound like the action is happening right now. Some readers love the immediacy of this. Others find it annoying. Present tense is less common in middle grade and younger books. Whether you use present tense or past tense, make sure you are consistent.

Exercise:

Pay attention to the viewpoint in the novels you read. Does the book use single or multiple viewpoints? First-person, third person, or omniscient? How does that work? Did you notice while you were reading, or did you have to make a special effort to check the POV?

Now I'm going to turn this book over to a couple of guest authors, for their views on whether it's best to use a single viewpoint, multiple viewpoints, or an omniscient narrator. First up, Nancy Butts shares posts from her Spontaneous Combustion blog.

POV Basics, by Nancy Butts

Viewpoint is often called point of view, which is where the acronym POV comes from. I will use all three terms interchangeably in this article. At its most basic, viewpoint means the character through whose eyes and ears, thoughts and feelings, a reader experiences a scene or event in the plot.

Think of viewpoint as if it were a pair of glasses. You as the author have the power to give these glasses to any character you want. Whichever character happens to be wearing those glasses at any moment in your book is your POV character. For however long that character wears those glasses – a sentence, a paragraph, a page, a scene, a chapter, or even the entire book – then you can write ONLY what that character can see through those glasses. The moment you switch from what the character is seeing, hearing, feeling, or thinking to someone else, even for just a moment, you have yanked the POV glasses off his face.

Here's an example:

Laughing at the TV screen, Ben crammed another salty handful of popcorn into his mouth. This show was so funny.

In these lines, the POV glasses are sitting invisibly on Ben's face. We know this because we can taste the salt on the popcorn along with him, and share his thoughts about why he was laughing. The line "This show was so funny" dips into his thoughts.

Now let's look at this next paragraph:

His father came into the room and scowled because the TV was so loud. "Turn it down, would you?" he barked.

The first eight words of the second paragraph are still in Ben's point of view. Through his POV glasses, he is seeing his father walk into the room with a scowl on his face. However, those glasses are yanked off Ben's face in the last six words of the sentence ("because the TV was so loud"). The moment I wrote the reason why Ben's father was scowling – because the TV was too loud – I left Ben's mind and jumped into that of his father, just for a moment.

It's subtle, but look at it closely. Unless this is a Stephen King novel and Ben is telepathic, he can't know why his dad looks so grouchy. When I wrote "because the TV was so loud," I jumped from Ben's mind to his father's. I changed POV, just for half a sentence. And that's what we call head-hopping, switching POV from one character to another too often, too quickly, or for too short a time.

Note: as soon as I quoted the actual words his father said, I jumped back into Ben's mind, because that was dialogue that Ben heard.

So how do you avoid the POV error? It's easier than you might think. All you have to do is rewrite the second paragraph like this.

His father came into the room and scowled.
Uh oh, Ben thought. The TV was too loud again.
"Turn it down, would you?" his father barked.

Instead of reading the father's mind, I stayed in Ben's head instead. From past experience – apparently Ben has been scolded repeatedly about the volume on the TV – Ben deduces that his dad must be angry about the noise, which is confirmed by the dialogue a moment later. But since I never left Ben's mind, writing only what he saw (his dad's scowl), what he thought (Dad's mad about the noise), and what he heard (Dad's command to turn the TV down), I've gotten rid of the head hopping. The POV glasses stayed firmly on Ben's face for the entire scene. The only way we find out for certain why Dad is upset is because he says so out loud, in a line of dialogue.

Single Versus Multiple POV

When you keep the POV glasses with one character for an entire scene or longer, that is called single viewpoint. That is the first of the three fundamental groups of point of view.

Note that in writing for kids, remaining in single viewpoint for the entire book is the norm, especially in easy readers, chapter books, and middle grade novels. There are variations with single viewpoint; you can choose to do it in first-person (I) narration or third-person (he/she) narration. Either is fine, so long as you stay consistent.

The second fundamental kind of POV is multiple viewpoint. This is when you transfer the POV glasses from one character to another. If you are telling the book from the perspective of more than one character, then to my mind, you're using multiple POV.

Multiple POV isn't recommended for children's books, though you do see it sometimes, especially in young adult (YA) novels. I think there are two reasons why single POV is preferable. First, it's less confusing. Remember, your readers are young. This means that they aren't just inexperienced with written language – they are also inexperienced with narrative techniques in fiction, so it's easy to confuse them.

Also, developmentally-speaking, kids have a more egocentric view of the world. Since each child sees herself as the center of the solar system of her life, it's easier for her to comprehend a book in which the young main character occupies a similar position.

What you hope to do in your book is bring your viewpoint character to life so vividly that readers start identifying with him or her closely – to the point where kids actually feel as if they are slipping inside the skin of the viewpoint character and experiencing every moment of the story with her. So every time you jump into a different character's POV, you forcibly eject kids from this character they've been inhabiting. And that poses the danger not only of confusing readers, but of alienating them as well. They might even put the book down and not come back when you evict them from a character they've come to know and love.

Use a tight single viewpoint to help readers slip inside the skin of the protagonist, to the point where kids can no longer tell where their identity stops and that of the hero begins. This enables kids to bond so closely to the hero or heroine that young readers experience and react to the events of the plot as if they were happening to them.

The second reason I think multiple POV is not the best choice is that it's very difficult to pull off, especially for a new writer attempting his or her first novel. It's a challenge even for experienced authors to do multiple POV smoothly and well. When you are first starting out, I think it's better to stick with single POV.

Connecting with the Character

Hypocrite that I am, I violated this single POV rule in my first novel, *Cheshire Moon*. I wrote from the perspective of a secondary character for a few chapters, which I felt was necessary to show how the protagonist, a young deaf girl, was (unbeknownst to her) sharing the same series of dreams with a boy she had just met.

But I used limited third person and stayed mainly in the head of my young hero in my second novel, *The Door in the Lake*. Is it a coincidence that this book has been much more successful than the first, earning an ALA Quick Pick and a Scholastic Book Club selection? I don't think so. I believe that my use of a single POV enabled kids to connect in a deeper, more immediate way with the protagonist, a boy who had mysteriously disappeared for two years and returned to his family with amnesia.

The middle grade novel on which I am working now has an even tighter focus on the eccentric young main character. It didn't start out that way. In the first two iterations of the manuscript, I was actually brazen enough to think that I could get away with seven – count 'em, seven – different main characters. Yikes! Fortunately, my critique group cured me of that particular delusion.

And they were right. When I allowed a young boy whom I had initially conceived of as a minor character to take center stage, the entire book came to life in a way it never had before. By focusing on his POV, and his alone, I found my way into the novel.

When children's writers decide what viewpoint to use, we don't just consider the needs of the story – we also stop to think how our choice of POV will affect readers. It's that perspective – the viewpoint of readers – that I think gets lost sometimes when writers discuss POV.

I think we need to realize that viewpoint is more than just a literary tool, a way to shape a book and showcase our virtuosity; we need to recognize how it's going to affect readers on an emotional level. It isn't just about us, in other words, and what we need as writers; it's about readers, too. And whenever we use the more distant forms of viewpoint, whether that be a shifting, multiple POV or omniscient narration, we increase the odds that readers won't be able to form a deep connection with our characters – and thus with our books.

At least, that's been my experience – not just as a writer, but as a reader. Perhaps it's all my years in children's literature, but I find myself increasingly impatient with novels where the author skips from the POV of one character to another.

Omniscient Narration

Which brings us to the third fundamental group of viewpoint, omniscient narration. Omniscient narration is when none of the characters in your book gets to wear the POV glasses: you keep them for yourself. Or for some invisible narrator who, in a god-like manner, knows all the characters inside and out. The omniscient narrator hovers above the entire book, knowing everything about both the characters and the plot.

The various forms of omniscient narration are less popular today than they used to be, though you still see it in fairy tales, fantasy epics, and in some picture books.

So there you have it. You won't go wrong if you think about the three fundamental kinds of POV in terms of who has the viewpoint glasses.

1. Single POV: One person has the glasses.
2. Multiple POV: Two or more people have the glasses.
3. Omniscient POV: Zero people have the glasses; a floating, invisible, all-knowing, all-seeing narrator's got 'em.

Nancy Butts never got over "The X-Files," as her middle grade novels *Cheshire Moon* and *Door in the Lake* both prove. (*Door* was an ALA Quick Pick for Reluctant Readers and a Scholastic Book Club selection.) She is also the author of *Spontaneous Combustion*, a why-to book for other writers; and a freelance book editor. You can find her at www.nancybutts.com or at her Spontaneous Combustion blog: http://chiralangel.blogspot.com/.

Multiple Points of View, by Christine Kohler

Now here's writer and teacher Christine Kohler, with a deeper exploration of multiple viewpoint.

In children's lit, editors prefer single point of view (POV) because readers identify more strongly with one main character. Children's and teen fiction today are character-driven, especially middle grade (MG) and young adult (YA) novels.

In some cases, a story may work best with multiple POVs. In that case, each chapter or section should still be told in a single POV, with a clear break when switching viewpoint. It's also best if the POV characters are alternated regularly, such as every chapter. Editors are concerned one character will be dropped too long and readers won't care about the character whose POV is dropped.

One challenge in writing multiple POV is to make the different voices and characters very, very distinct. Adding to the distinctly different voices, you can change tenses and/or person (first or third).

In Linda Sue Park's historical MG novel *My Name Was Keoko*, one sibling POV is in present tense and one is in past tense. I do something similar in *Gridiron Girls* with three POVS. The two football girls' POV chapters are in present tense and Missy the cheerleader's POV chapters are in past tense. The football kicker, Lupe, is Hispanic, so she does not use contractions in her speech – dialogue, internal monologue, and narrative – and her sentence constructions are often reversed since English is not her first language. Whereas in the quarterback's chapters, Dallas not only uses contractions but a strong West Texas dialect. By writing Missy's chapters in past tense then she can cover the same time frame as Lupe and Dallas' accounts, which are in sequential "real time."

Skinhunger by Kathleen Duey is a stunning YA fantasy novel in two POVs. Kathleen does a fascinating thing with time. I read this novel twice. The first time it took me partway into the novel to realize the one POV is past, leading up to the resurrection of magic. This is really hard to explain unless you have read *Skinhunger* because Kathleen does it in a way totally different than most present tense/past tense POVs.

The MG historical novel that possibly holds the record for the most POVs is *Bat 6* by Virginia Euwer Wolff, told in 21 POVs by two opposing girls' baseball teams.

Reasons for Multiple POV

My YA novel *No Surrender Soldier* is told in two POVs because the WWII soldier, Isamu Seto, is hiding in the jungle. In 1972, when teenager Kiko's story takes place, no one knows the soldier exists. If I had told the story in a single POV, then it might have still been suspenseful for Kiko to discover the soldier, but I would not have been able to show the reader how and why Seto hid and survived for 28 years in the jungle. Both POVs are in past tense since this is a historical novel. However, 15-year-old Kiko's POV chapters are in first person, whereas Seto's chapters are in third person. I wrote it this way so the reader could identify with Kiko, and not Seto. The third person puts a bit more psychic distance between the reader and the character.

In the YA sci-fi suspense novel *Now That You're Here*, author Amy Nichols uses two POVs, alternating chapters from a boy and a girl character. Both are in first person, present tense. However, since the characters are different genders, their voices are distinctly different. Here's how Amy arrived at the decision to write her novel in two POVs:

"I initially wrote it in a single first-person POV (the female character in the story), but found it very limiting. I switched to third person briefly, but that also didn't work…. Then I remembered how Lauren Baratz-Logsted wrote *Crazy Beautiful*, with two alternating POVs, and I decided to give it a try. The minute I started writing the boy's POV, I knew it was the right decision for this story. Because the characters are each experiencing such drastic and personal life changes, it made sense that getting both sides of the story and experience would make for a deeper, more satisfying read."

Notice that Amy wrote her novel in several different styles, trying out which worked best for her story. So don't be afraid to experiment, write and rewrite, until the characters are telling their own compelling stories – a story readers can't put down.

Christine Kohler, a graduate of the University of Hawaii, lived in Japan and Guam, the setting for her debut novel *No Surrender Soldier*. She has worked as a reporter, editor and copy editor, media specialist, school teacher, and writing instructor for the Institute of Children's Literature. She has 17 children's books published. Kohler now lives in Texas and is available for teaching writing workshops.

Learn more at www.christinekohlerbooks.com or follow her on Facebook: https://www.facebook.com/ChristineKohlerbooks or Twitter: https://twitter.com/christinekohle1

POV Exercises

• Remember a time when you were scared. Describe the event without naming any emotions.

• Write a conversation between two or three people of different ages from one character's POV. Then write it from another character's POV.

• Write the following scene using only dialogue and actions: Siblings have won a $100 prize. They want to use the money for different things.

• Rewrite the scene above, but change the characters' backgrounds. Make them richer or poorer, a different cultural group, or different ages.

• Write that scene again, from the first-person POV of one character, adding thoughts.

• Describe a character from her best friend's POV. Now from the POV of her ex or rival.

• Write about someone who drives you nuts, without saying how you feel. Use action, dialogue, tone of voice, facial expression and gestures, and your response/other people's responses. Try it in both first- and third-person POV.

POV Resources

Rivet Your Readers with Deep POV, by Jill Elizabeth Nelson

The Power of POV, by Alicia Rasley

Author Jordan McCollum has a section of downloadable free writing guides, including one on Deep POV, on her website: http://jordanmccollum.com/

POV 101: Get into Your Protagonist's Head and Stay There, by Jodie Renner: http://tinyurl.com/8klec4q

Diving Deep into Deep Point of View, by Rhay Christou: http://writersinthestormblog.com/2014/10/diving-deep-into-deep-point-of-view/

Chapter 5: Characters

Some authors prefer to start with a plot idea, while others start with an interesting character. Either can work, but ultimately the plot and character must work together. Let's start with a look at character development, as it intersects with plot.

A strong story needs conflict. Without conflict, you have one of those "slice of life" episodes that isn't a real story. But conflict doesn't just come from dramatic things happening. It comes from the character – what he or she needs and wants, and why he or she can't get it easily. Conflict comes from a character with a problem or a goal.

Let's start with a premise: a kid has a math test on Monday. Exciting? Hardly. But ask two simple questions, and you can add conflict.

- Why is it important to the character? The stakes should be high. The longer the story or novel, the higher stakes you need to sustain it. A short story character might want to win a contest; a novel character might need to save the world.

- Why is it difficult for the character? Difficulties can be divided into three general categories, traditionally called man versus man, man versus nature, and man versus himself. You can even have a combination of these. For example, someone may be trying to spy on some bank robbers (man versus man) during a dangerous storm (man versus nature) when he is afraid of lightning (man versus himself).

For our kid with the math test, here's one example: It's important because if he doesn't pass, he'll fail the class, have to go to summer school, and not get to go to football camp, when football is what he loves most. Assuming we create a character readers like, they'll care about the outcome of this test and root for him to succeed.

Our football lover could have lots of challenges – he forgot his study book, he's expected to baby-sit a sibling, a storm knocked out the power, he has ADHD, or he suffers test anxiety. But ideally we'll relate the difficulty to the reason it's important. So let's say he has a game Sunday afternoon and is getting pressure from his coach and teammates to practice rather than study. Plus he'd rather play football anyway.

We now have a situation full of potential tension. Let the character struggle enough before he succeeds (or fails and learns a lesson), and you'll have a story. And if these two questions can pump up a dull premise, just think what they can do with an exciting one!

Fears and Desires

As that example shows, conflict comes from the interaction between character and plot. You can create conflict by setting up situations that force a person to confront their fears. If someone is afraid of heights, make them go someplace high. If they're afraid of taking responsibility, force them to be in charge.

For example, my middle grade fantasy *The Genie's Gift* is set in the fifteenth-century Middle East and draws on the mythology of *1001 Arabian Nights*. It could have been simply a magical adventure tale, but the main character gives the story depth. She is anything but the typical swashbuckling hero:

Thirteen-year-old Anise, shy and timid, dreads marrying the man her father chooses for her. Her aunt tells her about the Genie Shakayak, the giver of the Gift of Sweet Speech, which allows one to charm everyone. Anise is determined to find the genie and ask for the gift, so she can control her own future. But the way is barred by a series of challenges, both ordinary and magical. How will Anise get past a vicious she-ghoul, a sorceress who turns people to stone, and mysterious sea monsters, when she can't even speak in front of strangers?

Because Anise is so desperate to reach her goal, she tackles challenges far beyond her comfort zone. This makes the dramatic action even more dramatic, while providing a sympathetic character and a theme about not letting your fears stop you from achieving your dreams.

You can also create conflict by setting up situations that oppose a person's desires. Sometimes these desires are for practical things. In my middle grade mystery set in ancient Egypt, *The Eyes of Pharaoh*, the main character is a young temple dancer whose one goal is to win an upcoming contest. When her friend disappears, she has to decide if winning the contest is really more important than helping a friend.

Perhaps your character simply wants an ordinary life. In my Mayan historical novel, *The Well of Sacrifice*, Eveningstar never dreams of being a leader or a rebel. But when her family, the government, and even the gods fail to stop the evil high priest who is trying to take over the city, she's forced to act. The reluctant hero is a staple of books and movies because it's fun to watch someone forced into a heroic role when they don't want it. (Think of Han Solo in *Star Wars*.)

Even with nonfiction, you can create tension by focusing on the challenges that make a person's accomplishments more impressive. In *Jesse Owens: Young Record Breaker*, I made this incredible athlete's story more powerful by focusing on all the things he had to overcome — not only racism, but also childhood health problems, poverty, and a poor education. I showed his successes *and* his troubles, to help the reader understand what he achieved.

To Build Conflict:

- Start with the character's goal. Create conflict by setting up situations which oppose a person's needs and desires.
- What does your main character want? What does he need? Make these things different, and you'll add tension. It can be as simple as our football player who wants to practice football, but needs to study. Or it could be more subtle, like someone who wants to be protected but needs to learn independence. (Or the reverse, someone who wants independence but still needs to be protected. Those two characters could even be in the same story. Life is complex, with many shades of gray, and books can explore that. Subtle concepts may be confusing for younger readers, but they are entirely appropriate for middle grade and young adult books.)
- Even if your main problem is external (man versus man or man versus nature), consider giving the character an internal flaw (man versus himself) that contributes to the difficulty. Perhaps your character has a temper, is lazy, or refuses to ever admit she's wrong. This helps set up your complications and as a bonus makes your character seem more real.
- Your character may change or grow as a person during the story. This is called a character arc. A character who changes is usually more interesting than one who does not. However,

growth does not always mean a reversal of attitude. The growth can come from reaffirming what the character already knew. For example, a child could know what is right but struggle to do it. In the end he does what is right, growing by following and reinforcing his beliefs.

• A character's growth can reflect your theme, by showing what the character learns. (More on theme in Chapter 13.)

• Before you start, test the idea by considering different options. Change the character's age, gender, or looks. Change the point of view. Change the setting. Change the internal conflict. What happens? Choose the combination that has the most dramatic potential.

• The conflict must be important enough to sustain the story, and it must not be too easy to solve. This will vary by story length and readership age group.

• It should take more than one attempt to solve the problem – three tries works well for shorter fiction. For longer fiction, add more attempts, or have each attempt made up of several parts.

• To build original plots, brainstorm 10 possible things that could happen next. Pick the least likely, so long as it makes sense for the story.

Some writers start with plot ideas and then develop the character who'll face those challenges, while others start with a great character and then figure out what he or she does. Regardless, remember to work back and forth between plot and character, tying them together with conflict.

A Note on Character Age

In general, children like to read about kids their own age or a bit older. They are not interested in younger children. That means if you are writing about the experiences of a five-year-old hero, your reader (or listener, for a read-aloud book) may also be five years old. If your main character is 10, the audience might be 8- to 10-year-old kids. Once in a while you will see a book with a main character who is younger than the target audience, but it's a harder sell.

Middle grade books are typically aimed at children ages 8 to 12. Often the main characters will be 12 or 13. Novelist Dianne K. Salerni is the author of a fantasy adventure series about a boy who discovers a secret eighth day, with people who exist only on that day. She says, "When my manuscript for *The Eighth Day* was submitted to an editor at HarperCollins, my protagonist Jax was 14 years old. Before bringing it to the acquisitions board, however, the editor reduced his age to 13. Later, she explained to me that age 14 was a No Man's Land as far as book stores (primarily Barnes & Noble) are concerned. If my main character was 14, the book would be shelved in the Teen section, where it didn't belong."

Young adult books are typically aimed at ages 12 to 18, although some have a narrower target, perhaps 12 to 16 or 14 to 18. Books aimed at teenagers with characters on the low end of that spectrum may struggle to find an audience. Many writers report being told to avoid characters who are 13 or 14. However, some recent published books do feature 14-year-old protagonists. Examples include Paul Greci's *Surviving Bear Island* and Robert Lettrick's *Frenzy* and *The Murk*. And in some series, such as Harry Potter and Percy Jackson, the hero ages from middle school to high school age.

While there are no absolute strict rules, try to keep your main character on the upper end of your target readership age.

Secondary Characters

When creating a new story, you'll probably spend the most time developing your main character. She is, after all, the star of your show, more important than any other actors. But don't neglect the rest of the cast. Major secondary characters should also be realistic, complex, and fresh.

In short stories or children's picture books, you don't have much time for developing complex secondary characters. Even in novels, chances are you'll have some minor characters who don't have an important role. It's easy to grab a recognizable "type" – the science geek, popular mean girl, bratty little brother. Because these types are so familiar, the reader recognizes the character with a few quick clues, saving time. However, beware negative stereotypes that are hurtful or reinforce prejudice, especially the ones based on race, gender, religion, size, and so forth.

You might also twist a character type to make your story world more interesting. Maybe you want your young heroine to turn to a grandmother for comfort. Easy – Gran is a sweet, white-haired lady who bakes cookies. We recognize the type, she fulfills her role, and such people do exist.

But she's hardly memorable. Think of the grandmothers you know. Some may be in their 40s, while others are much older. They might be retired or hold a variety of jobs. Their hobbies and interests could range from crafts to social activism to extreme sports. They may live alone or with a spouse or partner, other family members, a friend, or a professional caregiver. The real world is full of variety. Try making your minor characters as fresh and surprising as the people you know.

Maybe your fictional Granny dyes her hair black and gets donuts from the corner gas station. Maybe she's an archaeology professor whose house is full of strange artifacts. Maybe she's a bowling fanatic who consoles her granddaughter over bowling alley hot wings. Maybe she's an immigrant who only speaks her native language. As you develop her, some quirky characteristics may spark new story ideas. Regardless, Gran is now more memorable than that old cliché!

Causing Trouble

Your cast of secondary characters may include family members, friends, teachers, aliens, mythical creatures, or even pets. Some will be nice. Some will be annoying. Ideally, one or more should be trouble.

Even well-meaning secondary characters can make your main character's life more complicated. In stories for children or teenagers, loving parents may want what they see as best for their child – but if that's not what the child wants, it causes trouble. These challenges could add complications that interfere with the child's goals.

Examples:

In my middle grade Haunted series, Tania doesn't want anyone to know that she can see ghosts. She believes her mother would want her to contact her dead little sister, and Tania doesn't know how. Her stepfather would want to use her on his ghost hunter TV show, and people who saw that would think she was nuts. Her father doesn't believe in ghosts, so he might think she was lying to get attention. Family members with their own agendas make her desperate to keep her "gift" a secret, complicating her goal of helping the ghosts.

Milton Hershey: Young Chocolatier (written as M.M. Eboch) is a fictionalized biography about the man who founded Hershey's chocolate company. Milton's father was a charming dreamer who had big – but not good – ideas. He was directly responsible for Milton's businesses going bankrupt, more than once. Milton was only able to be a successful businessman when he learned to say no to his father.

Don't forget friends! One could turn out to be using the hero or secretly trying to interfere with his plans. Friends can have their own agenda, use the main character for popularity or access to something or someone, or secretly be trying to steal the main character's love interest. Even good friends can give bad advice, be competing for a spot on a sports team or the school play, or have their own problems which act as a distraction.

Example:

In *The Genie's Gift*, heroine Anise makes a perilous journey to find the Genie Shakayak and get the Gift of Sweet Speech. She starts out with her best friend, Cassim. But when he falls into a trap and nearly gets them both killed, he's so humiliated he acts like a jerk and demands they turn back. Anise takes off without him and has to make the rest of the trip on her own. Later, she's befriended by a kind caravan leader, but she has to protect her secret: she's a girl dressed as a boy.

Tip:

To see if you are making the most of your minor characters, go through your work in progress and list every major secondary character. What is their basic personality and role in the story? What do they want? Then ask:
- Could I make this character more interesting?
- How could these characters be causing problems, even if they don't mean to?
- If the character is already causing trouble, could those problems escalate?

If you don't have many secondary characters, consider adding some, space permitting, to add complications and drama. However, make sure any newcomers fit smoothly into the plot and don't feel like they are just shoved in to cause trouble.

And don't use too many secondary characters, especially for shorter work. Important ones should have a strong and consistent role. You can check an outline or draft by using a different color highlighter for each secondary character to create a visual map of how often someone appears. I did this exercise while outlining a middle grade novel. The main character was a 12-year-old boy. His little sister was important to both plot and theme, but she showed up in my outline mainly at the beginning and end. That warned me to include her in some middle scenes.

You can do this exercise with a complete draft of a novel as well, to find holes where you ignored a subplot or major secondary character for too long. You don't have to track characters who only appear once in passing, just those who have an important role. However, if you have lots of people who drop in and out, or several secondary characters who fill the same supporting role, consider combining or eliminating some of them.

Your main character may be the star, but major secondary characters also need to come alive. Think about their motives, their strengths, and their flaws. Add some surprising and contradictory qualities. Then let your whole cast of characters put on a fabulous show!

Character Tips

Start with the character's goal. The conflict must be important enough, and not too easy to solve. This will vary by story length and age group. Ask:
- Why is it important?
- Why is it difficult?

General categories are person vs. person (or group/society), person vs. nature, person vs. self (physical/mental/emotional weaknesses).

Six basic human needs influence character:

Security (safety, knowing the future)
Change (desire for variety, excitement)
Connection (feeling part of a group)
Independence (personal identity and freedom)
Growth (working toward a personal goal)
Contribution (feeling needed, worthwhile)

Create conflict by setting up situations which oppose a person's needs.

Building Strong Characters

- Heroes should be realistic, complex, and individual. Make sure your heroes have flaws. Even the people you love have flaws and irritating quirks. So should your characters. Think of unusual and contradictory qualities that will make for a fresh, unique character. Characters should have a mix of traits, good and bad, sometimes working against each other (such as a bright but undisciplined child).
- While they should be unique, heroes should also have universal emotions and motives. Readers should identify and sympathize to some extent, so they'll forgive the main character for their mistakes.
- Your hero should have the qualities needed to realistically overcome the challenge. Thus, the challenges should be hard enough to be dramatic (we must believe the hero could fail), yet not so great that no real person could solve them.
- In general, the protagonist should grow and change in the course of the story. She should make errors and learn something.
- The strongest stories have heroes with both inner and outer challenges.
- Protagonists should be active, not passive. They should take risks and responsibility. They may be at least partly responsible for their own problems. They should have to sacrifice something in order to succeed. This might be a tangible object (money, a toy, a prize) or something emotional (pride, safety, admiration).
- Heroes may be willing or unwilling. They can be outcasts, cynics, loners, wounded, or reluctant. But at some point they should commit to the challenge. It gets old watching a character try to avoid taking part in the story.
- Your hero's rewards should be proportionate to the challenges. An easy task should not receive an excessive reward. On the other hand, it can be unsatisfying if someone suffers through great struggles and receives little reward. The reward need not be treasure or fame, however. Saving the world, one's friends and family, or one's self can make for a satisfying success.
- Villains should also be well-rounded. A villain with good qualities and understandable motives creates a more subtle and complex story. Why is the villain nasty? Are they actually evil, or ignorant, or do their goals just conflict with your hero's?

• Other major characters also need strengths and weaknesses. Think about their motives, their good qualities, and their flaws.

Resources for Characters

Characters & Viewpoint, by Orson Scott Card

Dynamic Characters, by Nancy Kress

The Emotion Thesaurus: A Writer's Guide To Character Expression, by Angela Ackerman

Chapter 6: Plotting

An interesting character with a strong goal or problem is the key to a great plot. But developing that plot may take some more work. Remember, as discussed in Chapter 3: Developing an Idea, a plot has four main parts:

Situation: something difficult for the main character.

Complications: the situation should get worse, perhaps due to the main character's actions.

Climax: finally, the main character must succeed or fail. This is the last chance.

Resolution: generally, the main character should resolve the situation. The resolution may be happy or unhappy.

So how do you come up with all these parts of a story? Once in a while, a complete story may come to you. But often writers start with an idea that needs development. Here are some ways you can figure out the rest of the story.

Brainstorm. Jot down lots of ideas. Try using the plotting questionnaire below for inspiration. It can also help to get into a different environment. Take a walk, sit on your porch with a cup of coffee, or go to a local café.

Experiment with different writing tools. Some people like to use decorative notebooks. Others like yellow legal pads. Maybe using colorful pens or an old-fashioned fountain pen will help you. It sounds strange, but sometimes taking yourself out of your usual patterns will help free up ideas. I like to take a walk with a miniature digital tape recorder to capture my ideas. If your best ideas come in the shower, get some waterproof bathtub markers so you don't lose track of your ideas.

It's also helpful to have a journal and pen light by your bed, so you don't lose ideas that come from dreams. Keep a notebook nearby when you're out of the house, too, so you have a way to take notes in the car or while waiting in line. The best ideas can come in strange circumstances, and you don't want to lose them!

You can also try special brainstorming techniques such as a "mind mapping." A quick Internet search will provide instructions and examples.

Free write for ten minutes. This is a process where you write continuously, without stopping to think, for a set period of time. Don't worry about spelling, grammar, finding the right word, or even making sense. Simply write whatever comes into your mind, without pausing. It's best to set a timer so you don't keep checking the clock. Take a break, and then try another ten-minute session. Read back through your notes and circle or underline ideas that might be useful for your project. Do you have enough for a story? If not, try free writing again, focusing on developing what you have so far. Or switch to another technique, such as brainstorming answers to the plotting questionnaire below.

Brainstorm with others. Sometimes it's helpful to talk through an idea with other people. These could be friends, family members, or critique group partners. Writers are often better at seeing story possibilities, but great ideas can come from anywhere. However, only discuss your ideas with people who are supportive. It's important to avoid criticism, from others or yourself, at this stage. Some ideas will be silly. Others will be useless. Some might make no sense at all. When brainstorming, that's fine. The goal is to gather lots of ideas, not to analyze them. Negative opinions will shut down the brainstorming process. Be sure to explain what you want and need from your brainstorming partners. If someone makes a lot of comments such as "That's stupid" or "That won't work," avoid brainstorming with that person in the future.

Take breaks. Don't give up too quickly if the ideas aren't coming. Mull over the possibilities for a few days.

Outline. Use the plot questionnaire below. Brainstorm ways to fill in the blanks.

Or simply **start writing**. Write whatever scene is strong in your mind, even if you don't know where the story is going. Write about your character, or put him or her in a scene and see what happens. You can even interview your character or write a diary entry in his or her voice. You probably won't use this material in the final story, but it's a great way to get to know your character and to develop ideas.

Experiment – What works best for you?

Plotting Questionnaire:

Who is the main character?

Who or what is the antagonist?

Who are the other characters in the story?

What does the main character want? (What's the problem, goal, or greatest need)

Why is this important? (It should be vital to that character.)

What prevents the main character from reaching his or her goal? (The challenge can be a person, circumstances, society, or the character's own weakness. However, it should be something the main character can actively fight.)

What does the main character do about this?

What are the results? (Things should get worse, the problem more difficult.)

[Repeat the last two items several times]

What crisis finally results?

What is the climax? (Moment of decision.)

What is the resolution? Is the goal accomplished, or is it abandoned in favor of something else, or lost?

What is the theme?

Testing the Idea – what happens if you:

Change the character's age, sex, or physical characteristics
Change the point of view
Change the setting
Change the external conflict
Change the internal conflict

More Plot Tricks:

The inciting incident – the problem that gets the story going – should happen as soon as possible, but not until the moment is ripe. The reader must have enough understanding of the character and situation to make the incident meaningful. Too soon, and the reader is confused. Too late, and the reader gets bored and may not wait to find out where the story is going.

Increase the complications – at each step, more is at stake, there's greater risk. If each scene has the same level of risk and consequence, the pacing is flat and the middle sags.

Use the rule of three – the main character should try and fail at least twice before solving the problem on the third try. In long works, use the rule of three for each challenge.

If you get stuck on "What happens next?" try looking from the villain's POV. What are they doing to stop your character? What are other characters doing to interfere or add complications?

Up the ante – offer a better reward or more serious consequences.

A time deadline increases tension.

Give it a twist by adding new information that changes everything but still makes sense. (For example, Darth Vader is Luke's father).

More important and dramatic events should be written out, others can be summarized.

End with something dramatic and meaningful, whether exciting, funny, poignant, or sad. Don't ramble on after the dramatic ending, and don't end in the middle of nothing happening.

Plotting Resources

Advanced Plotting, by Chris Eboch

Beginnings, Middles & Ends, by Nancy Kress

Plot, by Ansen Dibell

Plot & Structure, by James Scott Bell

Scene & Structure, by Jack M. Bickham

An explanation of Plot Maps by author Lee Wardlaw, at the Project Mayhem blog: http://tinyurl.com/bv66ozf

Author Caroline Starr Rose provide an example of plot mapping: http://tinyurl.com/kb2tyod

Author Molly Blaisdell provides links to cool plot tools: http://mollyblaisdell.blogspot.com/2013/05/blooming-plot.html

Author Janet Fox's Diagram of Key Plot Points compares several different systems of plotting: http://tinyurl.com/lscpqfl

Author Dianne K. Salerni shares her plotting technique: http://tinyurl.com/kq4qxsq

Chapter 7:

Three Act Structure for Novelists

There's no magic formula for writing a fabulous book. But there *are* formulas that offer guidelines for constructing a satisfying plot. Scriptwriters have long used the three act structure handed down from theater, with additional "turning points" as guidelines for when high and low moments and surprises should hit. Various resources identify and name turning points differently, but here's a basic list of the most important ones:

- Act 1 (the first 25%): Introduction of the character and situation.
- The Inciting Incident/Catalyst (in the opening pages): Something that introduces a problem or goal for the main character.
- Plot Point One/Act 1 Break (about 25% of the way in): The point of no return, when the character embarks on the journey (physical, mental, or emotional).
- Act 2 (the middle, from the 25% point to the 75% mark): The character tries to solve the problem but faces escalating obstacles and rising stakes.
- Midpoint (in the middle of Act 2, at about the 50% mark): A moment of seeming success, but it may twist the story in a new direction or raise the stakes.
- Plot Point Two/Act 2 Break (at the 75% mark): The moment when failure seems inevitable.
- Act 3 (the final 25%): Wrapping up the story. Things may continue going downhill, and/or the hero(es) may develop a new plan, leading to the ...
- Climax/Resolution: The big final scene where the character ultimately succeeds or fails.

My brother Doug Eboch, writer of the movie *Sweet Home Alabama* and a scriptwriting teacher, says, "These ideas date back to Aristotle; they're not some new Hollywood formula. Three Act Structure is really just a way to talk about literary concepts. So, for example, the first act is the section where we set up the character, their dilemma and the stakes; the second act is where the character faces increasing obstacles to that dilemma; and the third act is where we get the resolution."

Following this format doesn't mean the result will be perfect, but, "If you understand the concepts, they can help identify and solve problems in your story, or even prevent problems from occurring in the first place," Doug says. "Think about acts and turning points as a way to organize your story and make sure you stay on track."

Many authors find three act structure helpful when writing books. Cece Barlow, author of the humorous teen story *Plumb Crazy* says, "I adhere to five turning points: the moment everything changes (in the first chapter), the decision that launches the adventure, quest, journey, search, etc. (in the third to fifth chapter), the point of no return (always at the mid-point), the darkest hour (70 to 80 percent in), and finally the climax (directly after the darkest hour)."

Most writers don't focus on structure at the beginning of a new project, however. Janet Fox, author of *Sirens*, a young adult noire romance set in the Roaring Twenties, says, "I need to let my imagination soar and not be constrained by any kind of road map during my first and sometimes even second drafts. When I revise more deeply, however, that's a different story. I really believe in the structure and in the importance of turning points, and need to impose that structure on my loose and random story. It helps to remind me that stories have universal elements that appeal to us all. Some of those universal elements are embedded in the structure."

Story structure can be used earlier in the process as well. Personally, I like to thoroughly brainstorm and outline before starting a novel. Matching scenes on the outline to traditional turning points is a way to identify weak spots or to discover when important plot points are happening too late in the story. This allows me to add complications or shift scenes around before I start writing.

Tools, Not Rules

Whether you start with plot structure or consider it only after a couple of drafts, checking your work for turning points can help ensure the story feels well-plotted and satisfying. But that doesn't mean you have to force a story to fit the "rules" precisely.

"It's more important to understand the concepts behind the structure than to take a fill-in-the-blank type of approach," Doug says. "Sometimes people focus on the idea that the act one turning point should happen on page 28 [in a screenplay, which is typically 110 pages]. But the reason we bother identifying an act one turning point at all is that it's the place where the hero takes on the problem and gets locked into the story. Without that, there's no tension because the hero could just walk away at any time. It's far more important that the act one turning point fulfill those requirements than that it fall on a certain page.

"Similarly, the act two turning point is the place where the hero seems as far as possible from what the final resolution of the story will be," he adds. "This is important because it creates suspense and unpredictability. For example, the act two turning point in *Sweet Home Alabama* is when Melanie, having gotten the divorce from Jake, repairs her relationship with Andrew and they begin planning their wedding. But by this point we've realized she's still in love with Jake. Of course because it's a romantic comedy, she will end up with the right person, but at the act two turning point it appears as though the opposite is going to happen. That's what drives the suspense of act three."

Know Why

As a scriptwriting teacher, Doug has many chances to see what works and what doesn't. "Many beginning writers get into their story too late. Often, they don't introduce the problem until the act one turning point and don't trap their character in the story until the midpoint. Again, this comes from not understanding the purpose of the beats." Those students are satisfied to find a big event at the appropriate place – even if it's not the right kind of event.

It's not enough to have *something* happen, just because you need a turning point. "Many beginning writers have major events happen at the turning points that are unrelated to each other or even the main character," Doug notes. "I see this particularly in stories based on true events, whether autobiographical or historical. The writer simply looks for the biggest events from real life and plugs them into the story beats in chronological order, rather than finding the events that best serve the underlying purpose of the beat."

While turning points may seem simple on the surface, they are not a paint-by-numbers solution to plotting. "They are not simply twists for the sake of having a twist; they serve a bigger structural purpose," Doug says. "All the turning points should be related to your main character and main story line and to each other. And each should be the result of the main character's actions and choices. So even if the second act turning point involves the villain getting the best of the hero, the villain should be taking that action in response to what the hero's done before. The turning points should grow out of what the character wants in the story and what obstacles stand in the way of that goal, including internal obstacles."

Three act structure isn't the only option, and even scriptwriting guides vary in how they list and explain structural turning points. Screenwriter Dan Harmon adapted Joseph Campbell's "Hero's Journey" into an eight-part circular structure, for example.

Janet Fox combines several structural techniques when revising her work. "I use a plot tool that I made combining 'The Hero's Journey' structure with Martha Alderson's 'Plot Whisperer' structure and mounted on a corkboard. I divided the corkboard into the three acts with masking tape, and added Alderson's plot diagram with masking tape, and I added the Hero's Journey points on a piece of tape up top to see where they fall."

Once she has that base, she says, "In my manuscript I mark each turning point to see where it hits the corresponding mark on the corkboard and the corresponding page count of the traditional structure. I use sticky notes, sometimes in different colors for different aspects of plot, character development, etc., to see if the scenes I've written are good turning point scenes, whether they change the action, and whether I'm increasing the tension. This way I can see visually whether I need to move or rewrite scenes, or whether I need to add a new turning point scene, all to maintain the overall loose but critical structure."

Keep It Natural

Regardless of which structural template you use, or how you adapt it, the key is to understand the purpose of turning points and make sure they fit naturally into your story. Writers can get into trouble if they add random twists whenever they reach a turning point. Twists should be the result of action leading to consequence. They should also be linked to character arcs, as someone grows or changes as a result of the action. Characters' motives should ring true. Your main character wants something, so she takes certain actions, which lead to consequences, possibly including more difficulties. She learns something from that experience, so she tries to solve the problem in a new way, and so forth.

A strong story may match the formula but shouldn't feel like it's following a formula. "I think because I write organically to start it's easier for me to not fall into the formulaic trap," Janet says. "After I've massaged the manuscript into the structure with turning points in more or less the right places, I use my later revision work to go back to my organic style, which introduces a new layer of complexity and further removes me from formula."

Janet adds, "For me a turning point works when the story truly spins in a new direction. It's subtle and hard to define, but when you reach a great turning point in a story you're reading you feel one of several sensations: 'ah, that's so unexpected'; 'oh, no!'; or 'of course! And now what?'. The best turning points urge the story forward with a sense of inevitable surprise. It's the paradox of pairing the unexpected with the absolutely right. I try to make my turning points places where the reader is surprised but also satisfied, because the moment is so sharp and thrilling and life-changing and true."

Exercise:

"To thoroughly understand each turning point," Cece Barlow says, "make it your practice to identify these points in every story you read. This practice will train you to understand what makes a turning point work."

Take notes when you watch a movie at home and see if you can identify the turning points.

Resources for Three Act Structure

Save The Cat!, by Blake Snyder, goes into more detail on plot points, while *Save the Cat! Goes to the Movies* uses examples of famous movies to show script writing technique. The Blake Snyder Beat Sheet covers important plot points in script writing, which can also be used for novels: http://www.blakesnyder.com/tools/

The Hollywood Pitching Bible, by Ken Aguado and Douglas Eboch, offers an inside look at script writing plus advice on developing great stories. Let's Schmooze is Doug Eboch's blog on Screenwriting: http://letsschmooze.blogspot.com/

Chapter 8: Beginnings

Previous chapters have given an overview of how a plot should work. The next three chapters will look at specific parts of a story: the beginning, the middle, and the ending. I'm largely talking about novels, but many elements will apply to shorter works and even nonfiction as well.

If you like to plan out a story in advance, and perhaps even outline, you can think about these elements in the planning stages. But you don't have to plan out or even understand all of these elements before you start writing. It's fine to write a story as it comes to you. Then after you have a draft, study these essays and see how the elements of your story fit. You may have to make major changes, but that's fine. It's all part of learning how to write well! Now let's get on to beginnings:

Making a Promise

Your opening makes a promise about the rest of the story, article, or book. It tells readers what to expect, setting the stage for the rest of the story to unfold – and hopefully hooking the reader's interest.

The first scene should identify your story's genre. For example, is it contemporary, historical, or futuristic? Is it a romance, a thriller, a mystery, a fantasy, etc.? Identifying the genre quickly can be trickier than it sounds. Say it's a teen romance, but the main character doesn't meet the love interest until later. Can you at least suggest her loneliness or desire for romance? (And get that love interest in there as soon as possible!)

Maybe you're writing a story involving magic, time travel, ghosts, or a step into another dimension, but you want to show the normal world before you shift into fantasy. That's fine, but if we start reading about a realistic modern setting and then halfway through, magic comes out of nowhere, you'll surprise your reader, and not in a good way. Your story will feel like two different stories clumsily stitched together.

If you're going to start "normal" and later introduce an element like magic or aliens, try to hint at what's to come. Maybe the main character is wishing that magic existed – that may be enough to prepare the reader. In my novel *The Ghost on the Stairs*, we don't find out that the narrator's sister has seen a ghost until the end of chapter 2. But on the opening page, she comments that the hotel "looks haunted" and is "spooky." Those words suggest that a ghost story may be coming. (The title doesn't hurt either.)

In my middle grade historical adventure *The Genie's Gift*, I originally didn't have any fantasy in the story until the fifth chapter, after Anise and Cassim start on their journey. But that seemed to set up the story as straightforward historical fiction. The novel opens with Anise's sister's wedding, which sets up the reason Anise leaves home. I added a scene where Anise and Cassim sneak into the kitchen to try to steal food from the genie cook. It made for a fun, active scene, and also introduced the fantasy world, complete with genies, right away.

Your opening should also identify the story's setting. This includes when and where we are, if it's historical or set in another country or world. Once again, you don't want your reader to assume a modern story and then discover halfway through that it's actually a historical setting. They'll blame you for their confusion. In a contemporary story, you may not identify a specific city, but the reader should have a feel for whether this is inner-city, small-town, suburban, or whatever.

Who and What's Up

Your readers will generally assume that whoever is prominent in the opening pages is the main character. Therefore your opening pages should focus on your main character. You may find exceptions to this rule, but switching focus can cause confusion.

You should also establish your point of view early. (To explore point of view, see Chapter 4 on the topic.) If you'll be switching points of view, don't wait too long to make the first switch. In novels, typically you want to show your alternate point of view in the second chapter and then switch back and forth with some kind of regular rhythm.

And of course, you want some kind of challenge or conflict in your opening. This doesn't have to be the main plot problem; you may need additional setup before your main character takes on that challenge or even knows about it. But try to make sure that your opening problem relates to the main problem. It may even lead to it.

In *The Ghost on the Stairs*, Tania faints at the end of chapter 1. Jon, who narrates the story, does not yet know why, but this opening problem leads to the main problem – she'd seen a ghost. If I'd used an entirely different opening problem, say stress with their new stepfather, that would have suggested a family drama, not a paranormal adventure.

In my Egyptian mystery, *The Eyes of Pharaoh*, main character Seshta is focused on winning a dance contest in the opening chapter. But her friend Reya hints that Egypt is in danger from some mysterious threat. She dismisses him at the time, but that hint leads to the main mystery after Reya disappears.

The Fast Start

So an opening introduces many elements of the story. Yet you can't take too long to set the scene, or your readers may lose interest. You want to start in a moment of action, where something is changing, and cut the background. But don't rush things. Take a little time to set up the situation, so it makes sense and we care about the characters and what's happening to them.

Fast, but not too fast. How do you find the balance?

You can test your opening by seeing how much you can cut. What if you delete the first sentence, the first paragraph, the first page? Does the story still make sense? Does it get off to a faster start? For a novel, what if you cut the whole first chapter, or several chapters? If you can't cut, can you condense?

On the other hand, if your beginning feels confusing or rushed, you might need to write a new opening chapter that introduces the characters and the situation. Try setting up a small problem that grabs the reader's attention, luring them in until you can get to the main problem. In my historical drama *The Well of Sacrifice*, the Maya are dealing with famine, disease, and marauders in the early chapters, even before the king dies and an evil high priest tries to take over. That gives readers time to understand these characters and their unusual world.

Don't stress about the opening during your early drafts, but do make sure you fix it later. Keep in mind that fixing the beginning may involve throwing it out altogether and replacing it with something else or simply starting later in the story. In the end, you'll have the beginning you need.

The First Chapter:

What is the promise of the first chapter? Set up readers' expectations:

- Genre (especially with fantasy, sci-fi, historical)
- Setting – time and place
- Whose story is this? Do we get to know and care about the main character?
- Premise – Do we get a sense of a problem? Is there tension?
- Tone – sad, humorous, action-packed, thought provoking.
- Do we get a sense of the structure of the book? – Does it switch between several interview characters? Does it include an unusual element such as letters or e-mails?

Make sure the book fulfills that promise, and that you have the right promise for that book. For a short story, try to include these things in the first 25%.

Some Fast Start Options:

- Start in the action, at a moment of change. Then work in the back story. (Back story refers to the fictional events that led up to this point, such as the character's past experiences, or the rules of the world in fantasy or science fiction.)
- Start with two people on the page. It's easier to have conflict with two or more people.
- Start with a scene, with action and dialogue. Use description and summary modestly, and only if really needed.
- Start in the middle of a fight or other conflict.
- Start with something powerful about to happen.
- Try starting with a small problem that leads to the big problem, or is an example of the main problem.

Resources for Beginnings

Start Your Novel: Six Winning Steps Toward a Compelling Opening Line, Scene and Chapter, by Darcy Pattison

Hooked: Write Fiction That Grabs Readers at Page One, by Les Edgerton

The First Five Pages: A Writer's Guide To Staying Out of the Rejection Pile, by Noah Lukeman

Author Keith Cronin explores strong starts at the Writer Unboxed blog: http://tinyurl.com/lzuac8l

Chapter 9: Middles

The middle of the story is where the complications happen. Your main character tries to solve her problem or reach her goal. But of course it isn't easy. She probably fails a few times, and the situation gets worse, perhaps due to her own actions. In a sense, this is pretty straightforward. But it doesn't always feel that way when you're writing! Maybe you can't figure out what happens next. Or maybe you're starting to realize you don't have enough material for a novel.

In general, there isn't a specific length a novel needs to be, but there are standards that fit the market. A novella might have a better chance of selling as a novel. Many teachers only allow kids to write book reports on books of at least 100 pages. Work-for-hire books (where the publisher assigns the topic and provides specifications) often require a specific word count. And then you have cases like mine:

"I love it," the editor said of *The Ghost on the Stairs*. "I want to buy it." There was just one little problem. I had sent in a 90-page manuscript for a middle grade series. He wanted 160 pages, to fit their series format for that age. "Send me the chapter by chapter synopsis on how you will rework it by next week," he said.

Of course I said, "Of course." I wasn't going to miss this chance to sell a whole series. But the manuscript already had a plot that worked well, with all the necessary elements. I wanted to keep the fast pace. How could I add 70 more pages, without getting repetitive or adding fluff that would slow the story?

I studied books on plotting, including *Beginnings, Middles, and Endings* by Nancy Kress, and came up with the following possibilities for filling my novel with more substance.

Add Plot

In my Haunted series, siblings Jon and Tania travel with a ghost hunter TV show and discover Tania can see ghosts. Once they figure out each ghost's story, they try to help her or him. In the original version of book 1, *The Ghost on the Stairs*, they find out who the ghost is quickly — the woman's name is already known, along with why she's stuck in this world grieving. The kids simply have to discover why her husband disappeared on their wedding day. To expand the story, I forced them to do more detective work to discover the ghost's name and background.

Tip: How easily does your main character solve his problems? Can you make it more difficult, by requiring more steps or adding complications? Can you add complications to your complications, turning small steps into big challenges?

Example: In Haunted Book 2: *The Riverboat Phantom*, a ghost grabs Jon.

I felt the cold first on my arms, like icy vice grips squeezing my biceps. Then waves of cold flowed down to my hands, up to my shoulders, all through my body.
I tried to breathe, but my chest felt too tight.
My vision blurred, darkened. The last thing I saw was Tania's horrified face.
And I fell.

That's dramatic enough for a chapter ending. So what's next? It would be easiest – for Jon and the writer – if his sister Tania is still the only one there when he recovers, and no one else notices his collapse. But if *everyone* notices, and Jon has to convince his worried mother that he's not sick, you get complications.

Tip: Use variations on a theme instead of repeating yourself. No one wants to hear the same old argument between your hero and heroine or see an identical example of your villain's villainy. But if you can add a twist, it will feel fresh.
Similar scenes should also go in order from easiest to hardest challenge, or with increasing stakes, such as time running out. If your main character has already become the hero in the big game, a casual pickup game won't be compelling now – unless he has a goal other than winning.

Example: In *The Ghost on the Stairs*, the kids make three trips to the local cemetery. The first time, they are with their mother in daylight. The second time, it's dark and stormy, and they're alone. The final time, Tania has been possessed by a ghost. Three cemetery scenes, but each different enough to feel fresh – and each scarier than the last.

Tip: Use cliffhangers, where a chapter ends in the middle of an exciting moment. Cliffhanger chapter endings have the obvious advantage of driving the story forward, convincing the reader to turn the page. But they can also inspire new dramatic events. If you have to find a way to add a scary or exciting twist at the end of the chapter, the following scene automatically becomes more dramatic.

Example: In *The Ghost on the Stairs*, I originally had the kids do research in the public library. They find information, and leave, with no drama. To keep the ghost more involved, I moved their research session to the hotel's business center. That allowed me to add this dramatic chapter ending.

[Tania] went out. I have to admit, I was glad to be alone for awhile…. It felt good to forget about ghosts and sisters and responsibilities, and just do regular stupid stuff.
Then I heard the scream.

By forcing myself to have a cliffhanger ending, I found some new and dramatic action for the next chapter. I also try to keep my chapters no more than 1500 words. If a chapter goes longer, I split it in two, which forces me to add a new cliffhanger halfway through the chapter.

Add Subplot

If you can't pack your main plot any fuller, try using subplots to add complexity and length to your manuscript. A subplot can add complications even if it's only loosely related to your main plot. For example, a kid solving mysteries may also be distracted and inconvenienced by struggles at school, a parent dating someone new, a friend moving away, or a host of other life challenges. As a bonus, giving your character a rich and complex life is more interesting and realistic.

(See the *Sammy Keyes* mystery novels by Wendelin Van Draanen for a great example of a kid character facing challenges with family, friends, and school, in addition to the mystery plot of each book).

You can also think about using one or more subplots to bring out your theme. A subplot can show the other side of the story, or delve into thematic ideas more deeply. If your main plot has your hero learning to be honest in order to develop a strong romantic relationship, a subplot might show her friend lying to win a guy, and then losing him. (See Chapter 13 for more on theme.)

Tip: Can you add or expand a subplot to develop your theme? To find subplots, consider showing other aspects of your message.

Example: In the alternate reality novel *The Amethyst Road*, by Louise Spiegler, Serena struggles against the dominant culture and her own tribal rules on a quest to control her future. She shares much of the journey with a young man, Shem, who is on his own quest. Both are rebelling against the expectations of their tribes, in different ways and with different goals. While helping – and sometimes using – each other, they develop a complex relationship. Shem's story enhances Spiegler's exploration of choice.

Spiegler explains, "The dynamics that occur between Serena and Shem allow the story to be multi-layered: not only an outward quest – through inhospitable territory and with difficult challenges – but also an inner journey, in which Serena's knowledge of her own heart and her own identity unfolds."

Use Secondary Characters

In the Haunted books, supporting characters include the kids' mother, stepfather, and the young production assistant who's supposed to keep an eye on them. These characters sometimes pop up at inconvenient times, causing trouble. But when rewriting book one, I realized I could use my secondary characters more.

In the short version, I had their mother offer to spend the next day with them, pressuring them to solve the ghost's problem the first day. For the expanded version, I included another day in the timeline, and Mom did spend it with them. They had to conduct their secret investigations with Mom looking over their shoulders, which added both tension and humor.

Supporting characters don't even have to be mean, or want to cause harm. They might simply have different goals. In the humorous YA novel *Plumb Crazy*, by Cece Barlow, the main character Elva takes a grueling summer job as a plumbing assistant so she can buy a laptop and pursue her writing dreams. It takes all she has to stay at the job for the whole summer, and she discovers she has way more grit than she thought. At the same time, Elva has two close friends, who have their own challenges with summer jobs and romance, and the three girls find their longtime friendship strained by their different goals and choices.

Tip: Look at your supporting characters one at a time. Could you use them more? How could they add more trouble for your main character? Could adding additional minor characters make the plot more complex?

Example: In *Freefall*, by Anna Levine, the main character Aggie is eighteen and about to be drafted into the Israeli army. She goes to boot camp to see if she has the strength, both internal and physical, to cope with the challenges. She trains with a group of girls and ends up befriending one of them. Their friendship, which introduces a subplot and a seemingly minor character, later becomes crucial in forwarding the plot as Aggie has to take risks for this friendship.

Levine says that though she did not plan on Lily taking such a major role in the novel, Lily became the perfect foil for Aggie. "Sometimes you need to let the characters lead you and you may discover ways of expanding upon the novel by exploring minor characters," Levine says.

Use Your Villain

Your villain's role is to make your hero's life difficult, right? Yet sometimes a villain sets trouble in motion and then disappears, twiddling his thumbs offstage while you focus on the hero's actions.

If your story action is sagging or you can't figure out what happens next, check in with your villain. Get him actively trying to thwart your hero, plotting new complications and distractions. By keeping your villain active, you'll keep your story moving.

In my Egyptian mystery, *The Eyes of Pharaoh*, I got to a point where I couldn't figure out what should happen next. The heroine had tried everything I could think of to find her friend, and she'd failed. Then I realized the villain knew about her attempt to expose him, so he'd be actively plotting against her. He drove the action in the next few chapters, setting up the main character's darkest moments.

Of course, not every book has an actual villain in the "evil genius trying to take over the world" sense. But even if you don't have a major villain, a minor one can cause trouble, either in the main plot or as a subplot.

In the Haunted series, each book's main plot involves the kids trying to help the ghosts. In *The Ghost on the Stairs*, I introduced a fake psychic, Madam Natasha. In *The Riverboat Phantom*, Madam Natasha figures out that Tania can see ghosts. Madam Natasha uses the secret as a threat, demanding Tania share information about the ghosts. In *The Knight in the Shadows*, the kids go to war with Madam Natasha, determined to expose her as a fraud. This is secondary to trying to help the ghost, but it adds complications and emotional drama.

Your villain might be a bully, a competitor, a nasty teacher, a difficult sibling, or a manipulative "friend." Whatever the villain is, his job is to make your hero's life miserable.

Tip: Consider your work in progress. Do you have a major villain? If so, is the villain as active as possible, aggressively trying to stop, hurt, or kill your hero? Do you have secondary characters with villainous tendencies? Can you enhance these, so they cause even more trouble? If you have no villain at all, consider adding one.

Use Setting

In my first version of Haunted book 1, the kids watched some of the filming, but I didn't use the TV show much. I added a chapter where they try out the ghost hunter gadgets, and another where their stepfather interviews people who have claimed to see the ghost. Both of these offered opportunities for humor, as only the kids knew whether the gadgets were really working and whether the interview subjects were telling the truth. As an added bonus, one of the interview subjects turned into a major player in the first three books. I created the fake psychic "Madame Natasha" on a whim, but I used her heavily in books 2 and 3, as she figures out Tania's gift and tries to exploit it. The setting inspired a new secondary character!

Tip: Look for ways to use your setting to add complications. What if the weather changed? What if they went somewhere without cell phone reception? What if they had to pass through a bad neighborhood or sneak through a rich gated community with a guard? If your setting could be Anywhere, USA, charge it up for dramatic value.

Example: Look at the movie *Sweet Home Alabama*. Would it be the same if the main character only had to go home to New Jersey?

I'm convinced that my changes made *The Ghost on the Stairs* stronger and more exciting, because I expanded the book by adding more meat, not just fat and gristle. The techniques I learned also helped me develop the other books in the Haunted series. Try these tips if you're having trouble making your manuscript long enough. Even if you don't need to target a specific length, these tips can help you pack more meat into your manuscript.

Chapter 10: Endings

Now let's look at how stories wind down: the climax and resolution.

The climax is the most intense point of the story. It's an exciting, dramatic challenge, where the main character must finally succeed in her goal, or fail with terrible results. You want the climax to be the most dramatic part of the story, so the reader walks away satisfied.

But before we get to the climax itself, let's look at the moment right before the climax. My brother, script writer Doug Eboch, points out that movie plots have a moment of apparent failure (or success). However the movie ends, "There needs to be a moment where the opposite appears to be inevitable. So if your character succeeds at the end, you need a moment where it appears the character will fail. And if your character fails at the end, you need a moment where they appear to succeed." (Doug's full essay is in my writing craft book, *Advanced Plotting*.)

I wondered whether Doug's point held equally true for novels. Looking through a few of the books on my shelf, certainly the climax includes a crisis point where the reader may believe that everything is going wrong and the main character could fail.

In *The Ghost on the Stairs*, Tania is possessed by a ghost and her brother Jon isn't sure if he'll be able to save her.

In *The Well of Sacrifice*, Eveningstar is thrown into the sacrificial well, a watery pit surrounded by high cliffs, and realizes no one will rescue her.

In *The Lion, the Witch, and the Wardrobe* by C. S. Lewis, the lion Aslan is killed and the good army is losing their battle.

In Eden Unger Bowditch's first *Young Inventors Guild* book, *The Atomic Weight of Secrets or The Arrival of the Mysterious Men in Black*, Faye tries to escape the clutches of the mysterious men in black when her parents seem to have completely abandoned her. She jumps from the car and runs but is quickly grabbed and brought back to be taken and deposited bodily, on the ground, outside the farmhouse. How can she possibly escape now, when the men are watching her closely?

In mystery or suspense novels, this may be the point where the bad guy has captured the hero or is threatening to kill him. In a romance, this is the point where the couple is farthest apart and we wonder how they'll ever resolve their differences to live happily ever after.

Does your story or novel have a crisis point, a moment at the climax where readers truly believe the main character could fail? If not, you may want to rethink your plot or rewrite the action to make the climax more intense and challenging. The happy ending is only satisfying if it is won at great expense through hard work. In literature as in real life, people don't always value what comes easily. Success feels that much sweeter when it can be contrasted to the suffering we've had to endure.

The Climax

Finally, at the climax, the main character must succeed or fail. You've built to this point with your complications. Now time is running out. The race is near the end. The girl is about to date another guy. The villain is starting the battle. It's now or never.

However you get there, the climax will be strongest if it is truly the last chance. You lose tension if the reader believes the main character could fail this time, and simply try again tomorrow.

In *The Well of Sacrifice*, the high priest throws Eveningstar off a cliff into a sacrificial pool. If she can survive and get back to the main temple in secret, she can confront the high priest with new status as a messenger from the gods. But the penalty for failure is death, the highest stake of all.

In Dianne K. Salerni's middle grade fantasy adventure, *The Eighth Day*, Jax has failed to protect his liege lady from being used in an evil ritual to destroy seven days of the week. The person he hoped would save them both, his guardian, has just been delivered bound and gagged for use as a human sacrifice by somebody Jax thought was on their side. Jax has one last, desperate idea, but his hands are tied behind his back and he can't implement it.

Movies are well-known for this "down to the wire" suspense, regardless of genre. In *Star Wars*, Luke blows up the Death Star during the final countdown as the Death Star prepares to destroy a planet. In *Back to the Future*, Marty must get his parents together before the future changes irretrievably and he disappears. He's actually fading when his parents finally kiss. In the romantic comedy *Sweet Home Alabama*, Melanie decides whom she really loves as she's walking down the aisle to marry the wrong man. The technique works just as well for books and stories, and you'll get the most suspense if the stakes are high.

This works for some nonfiction as well, especially biographies or memoirs. In *Jesse Owens: Young Record Breaker*, the book I wrote under the name M.M. Eboch, the true story had a natural ticking clock: the 1936 Olympic Games in Germany, where Jesse could prove himself or fail. In *Milton Hershey: Young Chocolatier*, also written as M.M. Eboch, Milton tried several businesses with financial support from his family. Each business failed and finally his family withdrew support. In the end, Milton had to succeed on his own, and he did.

Tips:

Don't rush the climax. Take the time to write the scene out in vivid detail, even if the action is happening fast. Think of how movies switch to slow motion or use multiple shots of the same explosion, in order to give maximum impact to the climax.

To make the climax feel fast-paced, use mainly short sentences and short paragraphs. The reader's eyes move more quickly down the page, giving a sense of breathless speed.

Exercises:

Study some of your favorite books. Is there a "ticking clock," where the characters have one last chance to succeed before time runs out? If not, how would it change the book to add one?

Now look at your work in progress, or a completed manuscript draft or outline. Do your characters have a time deadline? Do you wait until the last possible moment to allow them to succeed? If not, can you add tension to the story by finding a way to have time running out?

Happy Endings

The climax ends with the **resolution**. The resolution shows how the main character finally resolves the original challenge, and whether he changed or grew through the experience.

In almost all cases the main character should solve the problem or reach the goal through his own actions. Here's where many beginning children's writers fail. It's tempting to have an adult – a parent, grandparent, or teacher, or even a fairy, ghost, or other supernatural creature – step in to save the child or tell him what to do.

That's a disappointment for two reasons. First, we've been rooting for the main character to succeed. If someone else steals the climax away from him, it robs the story of tension and feels unfair. Second, kids are inspired by reading about other children who tackle problems and succeed. It helps them believe they can meet their own challenges. When adults take over, it shows kids as powerless and dependent on grownups. So let your main character control the story all the way to the end!

For example, Sam Bond's *Cousins in Action* series is an ensemble featuring five cousins who have international adventures. The children take turns at being the hero throughout each book. In *Operation Golden Llama*, three of the young protagonists find themselves kidnapped on a mountainside in Peru. Their eleven-year-old cousin outwits the adults and treks through the jungle to come to their rescue.

Child characters can receive help from others, though, including adults. In *I Am Jack* by Susanne Gervay, Jack faces bullying. He solves his problem, in part, by asking for help. In the end, Jack stands up for himself, but with the support of family, teachers, and friends. It's a realistic ending that inspires kids to take charge in their own lives.

This principle is equally important when writing for teens. Your main character should solve the problem. The teen thriller *Grift*, by Jason Mosberg, features a cast of orphaned teenagers living in Las Vegas and working as con artists for an adult leader. When a con goes awry, the kids must use their talents and wits to succeed in a dangerous adult world.

Even in today's romance novels, the heroine is more likely to rescue herself (and maybe the hero) than to let the hero do all the work. In *Plumb Crazy*, by Cece Barlow, the main character Elva wants true love. But instead of Prince Charming, she finds a pig farmer, a plumber with wandering hands, and the electrician Mitch McCall who criticizes her *Star Wars* fan fiction and accidentally cuts off his nose. She chooses to pursue her writing rather than boys, but she doesn't run Mitch off, discovering for herself love is just plumb crazy and Prince Charming need not apply.

Though your main character should be responsible for the resolution, she doesn't necessarily have to succeed. She might, instead, realize that her goals have changed. In *My Big Nose and Other Natural Disasters* by Sydney Salter, Jory starts out thinking that she needs a nose job to change her life. After a series of humorous disasters, Jory decides she really doesn't need surgery to feel better about herself. The happy ending then comes from her new understanding of her real needs and wants.

Stories for younger children generally have happy or at least optimistic endings, even if the original goal changes. Teen stories may end with an ambiguous or even unhappy resolution. Unhappy endings are probably most common in "problem novels," such as stories about the destruction of drug addiction. The main character's failure acts as a warning to readers. However, if you use this kind of ending, make sure your story isn't going to come across as preachy. And teen novels certainly do not have to have a tragic ending. Humor and action appeal to all age groups, and most endings are at least hopeful.

Tip: How the main character resolves the situation – whether she succeeds or fails, and what rewards or punishments she receives – will determine the theme. Ask yourself:

What am I trying to accomplish? Who am I trying to reach? Why am I writing this?

Once you know your theme, you know where the story is going and how it must be resolved. In *My Big Nose and Other Natural Disasters*, Salter wanted to show that happiness comes from within, rather than from external beauty. Therefore, Jory had to learn that lesson, even if it conflicted with her original goal of getting a nose job.

Chapter 11: Dialogue and Thoughts

I've read a lot of works in progress, between my work as a teacher through the Institute of Children's Literature, my editorial business, and occasionally acting as a contest judge or critiquing manuscripts at a conference. A manuscript with interesting characters and a fun, original idea makes a great first impression. But each scene has to be smooth, well paced, and exciting as well.

So what is a scene?

In writing, a scene starts when characters show up on the page and start interacting. A scene is a single incident or event, where you follow the action in chronological order, using action and dialogue (not summary). A scene ends when that sequence of events is over. Usually the next scene jumps to a new time or place, and it may change the viewpoint character. (See Chapter 4 on Point of View.)

A summary of events is not a scene. Scenes are written out in detail, so we see, hear, and feel the action. Imagine watching a play. The curtain rises and actors interact, moving and speaking. We feel like we're there in the scene with them. It wouldn't be nearly as entertaining if the curtain stayed down and a narrator stepped out to describe what was supposed to happen. Or it's like the difference between watching the play yourself, versus reading a plot summary of the play. Make sure your scenes feel like scenes from a play, not like someone describing a play you can't see.

A good scene typically has a mix of action and dialogue, with some thoughts and enough description to help the reader picture the setting. Some scenes are going to be mainly action. Others are going to be mainly dialogue. If that's appropriate to reality, that's fine. For example, people don't usually stop in the middle of battle to have conversations. Or you might have a character who is alone for a stretch of time, with no one to talk to. But in general, a story will be more entertaining and flow better if it has plenty of action and dialogue. Watch out for scenes that are all description, with no action, or all action, with no dialogue.

Thoughts as Dialogue

You can also use thoughts in place of dialogue. This helps keep the action from seeming like just a lot of stuff happening with no emotional reaction. Here's a scene from my middle grade Egyptian mystery, *The Eyes of Pharaoh*, where there's no dialogue. The main character, Seshta, has just dropped down from the roof after spying on people. I'll italicize the things that come across as her thoughts, to make them obvious. However, they were not italicized in the actual book. Also notice that I don't need to say "she thought." Because we are in her viewpoint, it's clear this is what she is thinking.

She paused under a willow tree to calm and arrange herself. She moaned as she smoothed her dress. Dust and little tears marred the fine linen, with one big rip in the hem. *How would she explain the ruined dress to the priestess?* She tried to cover herself with the shawl.

Most of the party guests still lingered at the far end of the garden. Musicians on lutes, reeds, and drums had joined the harpist. Seshta trudged past the pond. *What should she do next? She wanted to hear what Prince Penno said to Meryey, but they would be on their guard to make sure Miw's father didn't spy on them.*

Why was Miw's father there? What did the prince mean about "the other girl?" They hadn't said anything yet about Reya; she had to focus on him, whatever other strange things happened.

Notice how thought is woven in with action to show her reaction. In a battle scene, you might have fewer thoughts, but there could still be some, even if they're brief:

Richard is in trouble. Got to get to him.
That came close.
Duck!

Don't Forget The Reaction

In real life, we don't always know why things happen. In fiction, we should. We expect story events to follow a logical pattern, where cause leads to a reasonable effect. If you show a cause without an effect or an effect without a cause, you confuse your readers.

This goes beyond the cause and effect of major plot action. It includes a character's internal reaction to the external action. Yet I often see manuscripts where action is followed by action with no internal reaction, so we don't understand the character's motives.

No matter how great the action, the reader is confused and skeptical.

Within each scene, you need to show not only what your main character does, but also why. Don't assume people can read between the lines. In one manuscript I critiqued, the main character heard voices. Ghosts? The narrator never identified them as such. Did the boy think the voices had another source? Had he not yet decided? Maybe they weren't supposed to be ghosts after all. The writer may have assumed that readers would interpret this properly, but by not putting the narrator's interpretation on the page, she left this reader confused.

In *Manuscript Makeover*, Elizabeth Lyon suggests using this pattern: stimulus – reaction/emotion – thoughts – action. In other words, something happens to your main character (the stimulus); you show his emotional reaction, perhaps through dialogue, an exclamation, gesture, expression, or physical sensation; he thinks about the situation and makes a decision on what to do next; and finally he acts on that decision. This lets us see clearly how and why a character is reacting. The sequence may take one sentence or several pages, so long as we see the character's emotional and intellectual reaction, leading to a decision. You can vary the pattern, but make sure you include emotions and thoughts so your character's behavior is clear.

Dianne K. Salerni's shares an example from her middle grade fantasy adventure, *The Eighth Day*. First, here's the excerpt with action, dialogue, and description, but no thoughts:

Jax rode his bike into the center of town. The streets were empty. The traffic lights were on, but frozen green, red, or yellow.

"Oh, crap!" Jax yelled, braking.

It took three tries for Jax to break through the glass doors of the Walmart with a concrete parking block. He filled up a shopping cart with supplies he'd seen people grab before snowstorms or hurricanes and during zombie movies.

Without including thoughts, Jax's action doesn't make sense. Some readers might be able to guess why he's doing what he's doing, but others might be baffled, or they might guess wrong. Here's the actual scene (slightly edited for brevity), with thoughts:

Jax rode his bike into the center of town. The streets were empty. The traffic lights were on, but frozen green, red, or yellow. (Stimulus: what he sees)

He thought about zombies.

He thought about alien abduction.

He thought about the old movie where Will Smith and his dog were the last creatures on earth. (Thoughts)

"Oh, crap!" Jax yelled, braking. (Reaction/Emotion)

Will Smith and his dog had not been alone in that movie. There'd been other creatures that lurked in dark places and came out at night to kill. (Thoughts)

It took three tries for Jax to break through the glass doors of the Walmart with a concrete parking block. He filled up a shopping cart with supplies he'd seen people grab before snowstorms or hurricanes and during zombie movies. (Action)

Now the reader knows what Jax is thinking, how he's interpreting the situation, so his actions make sense. The scene is also more dramatic, with more emotion.

Writers often forget to include the character's emotional reaction and decision-making. We are so familiar with our characters that it's obvious to us how they would feel and why they would do what they do next. You just have to remember to put what you know on the page. My first draft of a scene often focuses on the action and dialogue. I read back through it intentionally focusing on the reaction, the character's emotional response, using both physical sensations and thoughts.

Make sure you're using action, dialogue, description, and reaction, possibly in the form of thoughts. Then you'll have vivid, believable scenes building a dramatic story.

Resources on Dialogue and Thoughts

Dialogue, by Marcy Kennedy

Adult fantasy author Michael J. Sullivan on dialogue basics, including how to punctuate dialogue: http://riyria.blogspot.com/2011/08/writing-advice-10-dialogue.html

Editor Jodie Renner on Some Dialogue Don'ts: http://crimefictioncollective.blogspot.com/2012/02/some-dialogue-donts.html

Scriptwriter Douglas Eboch on Five Tips for Writing Good Dialogue: http://letsschmooze.blogspot.com/2014/08/five-tips-for-writing-good-dialogue.html

Middle grade fantasy author Janice Hardy on Crafting Natural-Sounding Internal Thoughts: http://blog.janicehardy.com/2012/06/living-in-my-head-crafting-natural.html

Chapter 12: Setting

A strong setting can provide an interesting backdrop for your story. It may also teach young readers about a different part of the world or the different way some people live. But be careful about stopping the action to explain the setting in detail. Instead, try to work in details a few at a time, alternating with action, dialogue, and thoughts. Here's an example from my middle grade suspense novel *Bandit's Peak*:

The trail was only an old game trail, used by a few hunters during deer season. He wouldn't meet anybody, no hikers or early morning mountain joggers, nobody to ask questions or tell him he was too young to be out alone. He probably wouldn't see another person all day long. He smiled and his tension drained.

For a moment he thought of the days when he would hike and fish with his father. He shook the thought away. That was like another lifetime, when his father was a different person. It didn't bear thinking about now.

An hour later he reached the top of the mountain. He knew it was really a big hill, only 1200 feet high, but it was the tallest piece of land nearby. Down in the valley Jesse could see Main Street stretched in a straight line, heading past farmland and forests to other small towns.

Jesse turned, and the scene changed. Twenty miles to the east, Washington State's Cascade Mountains spread out across the horizon, some peaks still white with snow. You could lose yourself for weeks in mountains like those. Maybe he should try it. Just grab his camping gear and take off. Would anybody even miss him?

Jesse headed down a gully, scrambling over loose rocks and broken branches. Halfway down the mountain, he crawled over a tangle of fallen logs and met up with another trail.

He stopped and crouched beside the narrow dirt path. Footprints. Recent ones – not something he expected to see.

This includes a lot of setting, but that's not all there is. Readers see how comfortable Jesse is in a wilderness setting, which both shows his character and foreshadows later action in the book. You get a lot of Jesse's thoughts as well, which show his isolation and hint at problems at home. Finally, the footprints bring up questions and lead him to a dramatic encounter before the chapter ends. Earlier versions of the manuscript had several pages describing the mountain setting here, but I cut most of it to focus on elements that do more than simply show the surroundings.

Unusual Settings

Authors of historical fiction, fantasy, and science fiction should be especially careful to show life in action rather than pausing to explain it. It is tempting to describe and explain everything you know about the time and place, either because you are afraid readers will not understand the culture or because of your own enthusiasm for this strange world. But resist the urge to explain it all, and instead show the place through your characters' interactions. For my Egyptian mystery, *The Eyes of Pharaoh*, I tried to weave in details without stopping the plot:

Seshta ran. Her feet pounded the hard-packed dirt street. She lengthened her stride and raised her face to Ra, the sun god. Her ba, the spirit of her soul, sang at the feel of her legs straining, her chest thumping, her breath racing.

She sped along the edge of the market, dodging shoppers. A noblewoman in a transparent white dress skipped out of the way and glared.

In just a few lines, readers learn the setting (dirt street, market), cultural details (noblewoman), and religious references (Ra, the ba). But they are all conveyed within the action, as the main character races toward her goal.

"Show, Don't Tell" is a common piece of writing advice, and it certainly works for setting. "Showing" uses sense data, information perceivable by one of the five senses. It's what the viewpoint character can see, hear, smell, taste, or touch. "Telling" interprets or explains that data.

Janice Hardy, author of the middle-grade trilogy, *The Healing Wars*, says, "Showing allows the readers to lose themselves in the story. They can imagine what's going on based on the details and figure things out on their own, which is more rewarding than being told what things are. It's like the difference between being told about a new movie versus going to see it."

Whose Views?

Point of View is one of the best tools for showing since it lets readers see how the character experiences the world. (See Chapter 4 for POV basics.) Hardy says that learning to show "allowed me to get deeper into the heads of my characters, and thus craft a more immersive story. I wasn't just describing events like I was covering a sport and explaining the play by play. It made things more realistic, more unpredictable, and more enjoyable for the reader. They got to live in my world not just watch it from the outside. If you're solid in a character's head, everything you describe will be from their perspective. You'll be able to see the story world through that character's eyes and show what they see and how they feel about it."

The more unusual the world, the more important it is to show through viewpoint. "Point-of-view is the perfect tool for showing in a fantasy world," Hardy says. "A character will have opinions about what they see and the world they live in. Those opinions will influence how they describe the world around them, and allow the author to show how that world works by how the character interacts with it."

Often what you do not say is as important as what you do say. "A character who doesn't bat an eye while wizards fling spells around shows that magic is a natural part of that world and considered commonplace," Hardy notes. "Treating the sudden appearance of gods as normal occurrences shows that gods interfere and regularly make themselves known. The point-of-view character can make the fantasy world feel real to the reader by looking at it as they would see it. As soon as the author steps back and starts describing as they imagine it, that 'told' feeling can start slipping in."

When writing science fiction, fantasy, or historical fiction, you may occasionally want to show an unfamiliar attitude. For example, in my Mayan historical drama, *The Well Sacrifice*, the narrator describes her sister like this: "Feather was beautiful even as a child.... Her dark, slanting eyes were crossed, and her high forehead was flattened back in a straight line from her long nose." This shows the different Mayan interpretation of beauty.

Still, to be true to your characters you have to trust your readers to notice and interpret shown details. In *The Well Sacrifice*, I couldn't explain that the Maya didn't have wheeled vehicles, since the Mayan narrator wouldn't be aware of what her culture did not have. I could only show them traveling by foot or canoe. (You could discuss some of these things in an author's note at the end of the book, or in supplemental material for teachers posted on your website.)

Creating a vivid setting can be fun. But do not get carried away and try to include every item in a scene. Too many details get in the way of the story, so focus on the information or mood you want to convey. One or two details, shown well, should be enough to bring your scene to vivid life so your readers feel like they are there, seeing for themselves.

Picture Book Settings

This chapter applies mainly to novels, and somewhat to short stories and nonfiction. If you are writing picture books, you might not include setting details at all, since the illustrations can show the setting. Or you might focus on smells and sounds, rather than sights, to bring the other senses into the story.

If a picture book's setting is important, and not clear from the action and dialogue, you could mention the setting in a cover letter. You could also drop a few *brief* details into the text; they can always be removed once you have illustrations to show the scene.

A final option is to use illustration notes, which are directions on the artwork. These notes are usually put in brackets after the text for the page. They should be used sparingly so it doesn't look like you're trying to tell the illustrator how to do their job. One or two of these notes can help clarify things in the manuscript that might not be clear from the text alone. Here's an example from an unpublished manuscript:

Page 1: Sierra the Great Explorer hikes through a jungle. "I wish I had someone to explore with me," she says.
[illus.— giant potted plants make the jungle.]

Description Exercises

•   Write about entering a new setting that evokes a strong reaction (fear, joy, excitement, anger, pity). Don't name the emotion. Instead, show the reaction through sensory details – what you saw and heard, how you physically felt, etc.

•   Write a surprising reaction, such as a child terrified by a visit to Disneyland.

•   Describe someone sitting in a field, lonely and sad. Then describe someone sitting in a field, enjoying the day.

•   Write about a time when your health altered your senses.

•   Choose a location, such as a restaurant, bathroom, or cave. Describe it as a scene for a horror movie. Then make it a scene in a romance. Then a comedy.

•   Write an action scene (a chase, a fight) using lots of sensory detail.

Setting Resources

Setting, by Jack Bickham

Writing Vivid Settings, by Rayne Hall

Find three posts on setting on my blog:

http://chriseboch.blogspot.com/search/label/setting

Chapter 13. Theme

Theme, in writing, is the message or moral of the story. Every story has a message. Even a tall tale about giant lumberjack Paul Bunyan, filled with humorous exaggeration, might show how hard work and resolve overcome all obstacles. Nonfiction topics also have themes. For example, a biography might portray courage in the face of danger, perseverance despite many setbacks, or the value of creative thinking. Even poetry can have a theme. A haiku about a tree shares a theme about the beauty of nature.

Theme expresses an opinion on the world. Concepts such as family, racism, or world peace are not themes. They are topics; the theme is what you have to say about that topic. If you are writing about world peace, is your message simply that peace would be good? That it's impossible? It's something we each need to work for as individuals? It can only be achieved through the guidance of religion? It can only be achieved if we give up religion, which causes people to think their way is better than others? Different individuals could have a wide variety of messages on the topic of world peace.

Theme is important because a strong theme turns a story into more than a few minutes or hours of distraction. Theme can change us as people. Perhaps a young reader is inspired to stand up against injustice, or to follow her dream.

However, a story's theme should not be too obvious. One of the first lessons children's writers hear is "Don't preach." Children read for fun, not a lecture, so you shouldn't end your stories with obvious morals. The message should come out through the story itself, from the thoughts and actions of the main character, and what she learned from the experience. Instead, many beginning writers make their theme too obvious. Perhaps an adult character scolds the child, telling him how he should have behaved. Or the writer flatly states the moral at the end, like an Aesop's fable. Don't do that. Keep the message subtle.

Vague Themes

Some writers, even advanced ones, suffer from a different thematic challenge. The theme may be unclear, perhaps even to the writer herself.

Young adult author Holly Cupala says, "Throughout the writing of *Tell Me A Secret*, I would hit on something and think, This is the theme! Then a little later, No, *this* is the theme. It seems to be an evolving – or perhaps devolving – process, getting to the heart of the story, layer by layer. I even found an old blog of mine where I thought I'd hit on the theme and had the same experience – the chills, the thunderous weight of the moment you realize, 'Wait, wait, wait. *This* is the theme.' I think on some level I've been right every time, chipping away at the complex layers of what it means to write something as truthfully as possible."

As this successful novelist shows, you don't always have to know your theme before you start. Sometimes, you may discover your message as you write the story. Or you may start with one idea in mind, and change it as you go. You may even realize that you don't quite believe your original theme – writing the story may help you explore new aspects of that idea, uncovering complexities and contradictions. This can result in a deeper, more meaningful story, so let that process unfold.

Uma Krishnaswami says of her middle grade novel, "I did not know the theme of *Naming Maya* until I was through the fifth draft. I never thought of it as theme, even then, because words like 'theme' that come from literary criticism rather than craft tend to shut me down. Instead I spent a lot of time asking myself, 'What is this story really about? What does Maya long for?' She thinks she wants her father back but that wasn't the want that drove the book. I wrote myself fake jacket blurbs, trying to get at that elusive heart. By that time I was well into my sixth draft. The thematic through-line of identity emerged quite suddenly one day. Truthfully, I am not sure that we should be thinking too much, too soon, about theme. It's a fragile concept, and we need to allow it to come out of the subconscious mind, which is where the best writing takes place. In my opinion, when themes are planted in place too intentionally, stories come across as heavy-handed and with the author's stamp far too clearly imprinted."

Focusing too much on a specific theme at the beginning can result in stiff characters, a clunky plot, and that dreaded preaching. But you should know your theme before you finish your final draft. That way you can edit to make sure your story best supports your theme.

My World View

When trying to identify your theme, start big and then narrow your focus. Can you define your theme in one word? Is it about love, hope, courage, sacrifice? Once you've identified that word, try to state your theme as a single, clear sentence. What do you want to say about that word? For example, if your novel is about sacrifice, what about it? Is your character making sacrifices for her own future, for a loved one, for her country, for an ideal? What does she have to sacrifice? Narrowing in on the specifics can help you pinpoint your theme.

Once you've clarified your theme, work backward. Does your story truly support it? Maybe you've decided that your theme is "The greater good is more important than the individual's desire." In that case, your main character should be giving up a desire in order to help a larger group. But perhaps you liked your character so much that you ended with her helping the group and getting what she wanted as well. That weakens your message, and suggests a different theme, "Good will be rewarded." You might want to reconsider your ending.

Try to envision all the different messages someone could get from your story. I read one unpublished manuscript about a bee who is ostracized because he can't buzz. When honey is stolen, the young bee silently tracks the thief, proving himself to the community. The writer wanted to say that everyone has special qualities. Instead, her story could suggest that you won't be accepted unless you prove yourself through heroic action. That might encourage kids to look for ways to show off, rather than to accept themselves as they are.

Having readers miss your intended theme can become a big problem. I've read manuscripts about bullying that seemed to suggest the answer to being bullied is to placate the bully or lie to adults on his behalf. I can't imagine these stories being published. Find a few people to read your story – especially young people, if possible – and ask them what message they take away. Make sure their response is in line with your ideals.

Don't expect your readers to pick out your theme exactly, however. If they do, you're probably not being subtle enough. Just make sure they find a valuable message. In my Mayan adventure, *The Well of Sacrifice*, I knew my main theme: make your own decisions and stand up for your beliefs. My heroine, Eveningstar, learns that she can't depend on her heroic older brother, her parents, the government, or religion to solve the city's problems. When they all fail her, she has to act by herself.

One young reader wrote me and said, "The book ... helped me think to never give up, even in the worst of times, just like what happened to Eveningstar." I'm happy to inspire a reader to "never give up," even if that wasn't my main theme. And perhaps readers will be subtly influenced by my primary message, even if they don't recognize it while reading.

Too Many Messages?

For younger readers and short stories, keep the theme simple. The longer the story or novel, and the older the reader, the more complex you can be. At first a book may appear to be a humorous romance, but as the story unfolds, it may reveal a theme about honesty in relationships.

Your theme doesn't have to be obvious from your first paragraph, and probably shouldn't be. In fact, the theme may only be clear from the final twist in the story. The theme can be revealed through what the main character learns, how she changes, what she gains or loses.

As part of your revisions (or in the planning stage, if you are really organized), work on your character in order to set up your theme. Use her virtues and vices. How will her strengths help her? What weaknesses does she have to overcome? Make sure these tie into the theme. If your character must learn about honesty, make sure that it will be possible but difficult for her. Maybe she craves intimacy, but is afraid no one will like her if she shows her true self.

For longer works, think about how you can use other characters or subplots to support or expand on your theme. Maybe your teen main character learns to be honest in her relationships, and so develops a loving connection with her boyfriend. In contrast, her friend might keep lying in order to make a good impression, and get dumped, or wind up with a shallow, dissatisfying relationship. A subplot with the main character's divorced parents could explore the theme in yet another way.

Although it's useful to identify a single main theme, you may have additional themes. Holly Cupala says, "The themes I seem to be writing are identity and memory and how they intersect. It's very much there in the novel I'm working on now. Then there are the peripheral themes – looking to the past for meaning versus looking to the future for purpose, trying to find yourself in others, wanting to be loved for who you are, blaming versus hoping." She notes that the themes are there in *Don't Breathe a Word*, her second novel, as well as her work in progress, tentatively titled *I'll Never Tell*.

Multiple themes can give a novel extra depth and power. However, don't let your story get cluttered with too many themes, especially wildly different ones. If you try to share everything you believe about life in one story, it will feel cluttered and confusing. Focus on one primary theme, and save the others for different works.

Nonfiction Truths

Identifying a theme can even help in writing powerful nonfiction. Christine Liu-Perkins, author of *At Home in Her Tomb: Lady Dai and the Ancient Chinese Treasures of Mawangdui*, says, "My book is about a set of 2,100-year-old tombs in China that had over 3,000 well-preserved artifacts, including the body of a woman. I decided to write about the tombs as a time capsule, the various artifacts revealing what life was like during that period. Coming up with a theme really helped me develop the focus and content for my nonfiction book, and also helped in pitching my proposal to the publisher."

Shirley Raye Redmond gives another example from a nonfiction picture book. "Before writing my first draft of *Blind Tom: The Horse Who Helped Build the Great Railroad*, I narrowed the focus of my story and identified my story theme by answering the following questions as thoroughly as possible: who, what, when, where, how, and why? I then abbreviated my answers so they fit concisely on an index card. On the back of the card, I wrote my theme statement: *With perseverance, ordinary people (and even a blind horse) can play important roles in shaping major historical events*. I kept my 'focus card' where I could see it as I drafted – and later refined – my story."

For my fictionalized biography of Olympic runner Jesse Owens, I considered the various lessons of his life in order to focus the book. Because he overcame ill health, racism, poverty, and a poor education to become one of the greatest athletes the world has known, a theme quickly presented itself: Suffering can make you stronger, if you face it with courage and determination. With this in mind, I chose to open the book when Jesse was five, and his mother cut a growth from his chest with a knife. I ended the chapter with his father saying, "If he survived that pain, he'll survive anything life has to offer. Pain won't mean nothing to him now." Jesse shows that spirit again and again throughout *Jesse Owens: Young Record Breaker* (written under the name M. M. Eboch). Identifying that theme helped me craft a dramatic story, one that may even inspire kids to tackle their greatest challenges.

In your theme, you can find the heart of your story. It's your chance to share what you believe about the world, so take the time to identify and clarify your theme, and make sure your story supports it. Through your messages, you may influence children, and perhaps even change lives.

Theme Tips

To identify your theme, ask yourself:

- What is this story really about?

- What does my main character long for?

- What is the desire that drives the story?

Start big and then narrow your focus.

- Can you define your theme in one word? Is it about love, hope, courage, sacrifice?

- What do you want to say about that word? For example, if your novel is about sacrifice, what about it? Is your character making sacrifices for her own future, for a loved one, for her country, for an ideal? What does she have to sacrifice? Narrowing in on the specifics can help you pinpoint your theme.

Write down your theme in a single, clear sentence.

Then ask yourself – How can I further clarify or explore this theme?

- What does the main character learn? How does she change? What does she gain or lose?

- How will her strengths help her? What weaknesses does she have to overcome? Make sure that it will be possible but difficult for her to learn the lesson.

- For longer works, how can you use other characters or subplots to support or expand on your theme?

Chapter 14: Editing

The book market is more competitive than ever. Editors with mile-high submission piles can afford to choose only exceptional manuscripts. Authors who self-publish must produce work that is equal to releases from traditional publishers. And regardless of their publishing path, authors face competition from tens of thousands of other books. Serious authors know they must extensively edit and polish their manuscripts.

If you're not trying to publish your work, or if you're self-publishing for family and friends and don't care about sales, you don't have to worry as much about editing. However, if you want to write a great book – no matter what future you see for it – then editing is still key. Plus, you'll learn a lot about writing, which will help you on future manuscripts.

For many writers, a new manuscript is their "baby." You love it, and it may be hard to think of it as anything less than perfect. But you wouldn't send your newborn baby out into the world and expect it to survive on its own. You help your children grow up, teaching them, gently correcting misbehavior, and helping them express their wonderful selves. As your children grow older, you can step back a bit and see them as individuals in their own right, separate from you. Once they are grown, you can send them off into the world, perhaps still worrying at times but with confidence that they can survive on their own.

Editing a manuscript is similar. You need to distance yourself enough from the work that you can see it for what it is – not what you dreamed it would be, but what is actually on the page. Then you guide and shape it, perhaps with help from others. You release it into the world when you're confident the story can survive on its own, without you there to explain or defend it.

The Big Picture

Wading through hundreds of novel pages trying to identify every problem at once is intimidating and hardly effective. Even editing a picture book, short story, or article can be overwhelming if you try to address every issue at once. The best self-editors break the editorial process into steps. They also develop practices that allow them to step back from the manuscript and see it as a whole.

Editor Jodie Renner recommends putting your story away for a few weeks after your first complete draft. During that time, share it with a critique group or beta readers. (Beta readers give feedback on an unpublished draft. They are not necessarily writers, so they give a reader's opinion.) Ask your advisors to look only at the big picture: "where they felt excited, confused, curious, delighted, scared, worried, bored, etc.," Renner says. During your writing break, you can also read books, articles, or blog posts to brush up on your craft techniques.

Then collect the feedback and make notes, asking for clarification as needed. Consider moving everyone's comments onto a single manuscript for simplicity. This also allows you to see where several people have made similar comments, and to choose which suggestions you will follow. At this point, you are only making notes, not trying to implement changes.

In my book *Advanced Plotting*, I suggest making a chapter by chapter outline of your manuscript so you can see what you have without the distraction of details. For each scene or chapter, note the primary action, important subplots, and the mood or emotions. By getting this overview of your novel down to a few pages, you can go through it quickly looking for trouble spots. You can compare your outline to The Hero's Journey or scriptwriting three-act structure to see if those guidelines inspire any changes. (Look up either phrase on the Internet for more information, or see Chapter 7 for information on three act structure.)

As you review your scenes, pay attention to anything that slows the story. Where do you introduce the main conflict? Can you eliminate your opening chapter(s) and start later? Do you have long passages of back story or explanation that aren't necessary? Does each scene have conflict? Are there scenes out of order or repetitive scenes that could be cut? Make notes on where you need to add new scenes, delete or condense boring scenes, or move scenes.

Colored highlighter pens (or the highlight function on a computer) can help you track everything from point of view changes to clues in a mystery to thematic elements. Highlight subplots and important secondary characters to make sure they are used throughout the manuscript in an appropriate way. Cut or combine minor characters who aren't necessary.

Using Your Notes

Once you have an overview of the changes you want, revise the manuscript for these big picture items: issues such as plot, structure, characterization, point of view, and pacing. Renner recommends you then reread the entire manuscript, still focusing on the big picture. Depending on the extent of your changes, you may want to repeat this process several times.

During this stage of editing, consider market requirements if you plan to submit the work to publishers. Is your word count within an appropriate range for the genre? Are you targeting a publisher that has specific requirements? If you're writing a romance, will the characters' arcs and happy ending satisfy those fans? If you have an epic fantasy, is the world building strong and fresh? If your thriller runs too long, can it be broken into multiple books, or can you eliminate minor characters and subplots?

Once you've done all you can, you may want to hire an editor. The next chapter, on Critiques, discusses using professional editors. You could also send the manuscript to new beta readers or critique partners. People who have not read the manuscript before might be better at identifying how things are working now.

Fine Tuning

Once you are confident that your characters, plot, structure, and pacing are working, you can dig into the smaller details. At this stage, make sure that your timeline works and your setting hangs together. Create calendars and maps to keep track of when things happen and where people go. Then polish, polish, polish.

Bill Peschel, author of Sherlock Holmes parodies and other books for adults, and a former newspaper copy editor, says, "Reading with a critical eye reveals weak spots in grammar, consistently misspelled words, and a reliance on 'crutch words' [unnecessary and overused words] such as *simply*, *basically*, or *just*. While it can be disheartening to make the same mistakes over and over again, self-editing can boost your ego when you become aware that you're capable of eliminating them from your work. It takes self-awareness, some education, and a willingness to admit to making mistakes."

This stage of editing can be time-consuming, especially if you are prone to spelling or grammatical errors. "Be systematic," Peschel says. "Despite all the advice on how to multi-task, the brain operates most efficiently when it's focusing on one problem at a time. This applies to proofing. You can look for spelling mistakes, incorrect grammar, and your particular weaknesses, just not at the same time. So for effective proofing, make several passes, each time focusing on a different aspects."

One pass might focus only on dialogue. "Read just the dialogue out loud," Renner suggests, "maybe role-playing with a buddy or two. Do the conversations sound natural or stilted? Does each character sound different, or do they all sound like the author?"

Wordiness (using more words than necessary) is a big problem for many writers, so make at least one pass focused exclusively on tightening. "Make every word count," Renner advises. "Take out whole sentences and paragraphs that don't add anything new or drive the story forward. Take out unnecessary little words, most adverbs and many adjectives, and eliminate clichés." Words you can almost always cut include very, really, just, sort of, kind of, a little, rather, started to, began to, then. To pick up the pace in your manuscript, try to cut 20% of the text on every page, simply by looking for unnecessary words or longer phrases that can be changed to shorter ones.

Make additional passes looking for grammar errors, missing words, and your personal weak areas. For example, if you know you tend to overuse "just," use the "Find" option in a program like Microsoft Word to locate that word and eliminate it when possible.

Even if you're not an expert editor, you may be able to sense when something is wrong. "Trust your inner voice," when you get an uneasy feeling, Peschel says. "It can be something missing, something wrong, something clunky, and if you stick to it – read it out loud, read it backwards, look at it from a distance – the mistake should declare itself."

Fool Your Brain

By this point, you've read your manuscript dozens of times. This can make it hard to spot errors, since you know what is *supposed* to be there. Several tricks can help you see your work with fresh eyes.

Peschel says, "Reading the same prose in the same font can cause the eye to skate over mistakes, so change it up. Boost the size or change the color of the text or try a different font. Use free programs such as Calibre or Scrivener to create an EPUB or MOBI file that can be read on an ebook reader."

Renner also recommends changing your font. Print your manuscript on paper if you are used to working on the computer screen. Finally, move away from your normal working place to review your manuscript. "These little tricks will help you see the manuscript as a reader instead of as a writer," she says.

"An effective way to check the flow of your story is to read it aloud or have someone read it to you," freelance editor Linda Lane notes. "Better yet, record your story so you can play it back multiple times if necessary. Recruiting another person to do this will give you a better idea of what a reader will see." Some software, such as MS Word 2010, has a text-to-voice feature to provide a read aloud. Lane adds, "If recording your story yourself, run your finger just below each line as you read to catch omitted or misspelled words and missing commas, quote marks, and periods. Also, enunciate clearly and 'punctuate' as you read, pausing slightly at each comma and a bit longer at end punctuation. While this won't catch every error, it will give you a good sense of flow, highlight many shortcomings, and test whether your dialogue is smooth and realistic."

Some people even recommend reading your manuscript backwards, sentence by sentence. While this won't help you track the flow of the story, it focuses attention on the sentence level. Finally, certain computer programs and web platforms are designed to identify spelling and grammar errors, and in some cases even identify clichés. While these programs are not recommended for developmental editing (when you're shaping the story), they can be an option for later polishing. (They can also make mistakes, though, so don't trust Microsoft Word's spelling & grammar check to be right about everything.)

How Much Is Enough?

How much editing you need to do depends on your goals for the story. If you simply want to write down the bedtime stories you tell your children as a family record, a spelling error or two doesn't matter too much. If you are going to submit work to a publisher, you need to be more careful. Some editors and agents say they will stop reading if they find errors in the first few pages, or more than one typo every few pages. If you plan to self-publish, most experts advise hiring a professional editor to help you shape the story and a professional proofreader to make sure the book doesn't go out with typos. Weak writing and other errors could cause readers to get annoyed and leave bad reviews.

Looking at all the steps to successful self-editing may be daunting, but break them down into pieces, take a step at a time, and don't rush your revisions. "This whole process could easily take several months," Renner says. "Don't shoot yourself in the foot by putting your manuscript out too soon."

Each time you go through this process you'll be developing your skills, making the next time easier. "Like anything else, self-editing becomes easier the more you do it," Peschel says. "When it becomes second-nature, you'll have made a big leap toward becoming a professional writer."

Editing Tips:

Don't try to edit everything at once. Make several passes, looking for different problems. Start big, then focus in on details.

Try writing a one- or two-sentence synopsis. Define your goal. Do you want to produce an action-packed thriller? A laugh-out-loud book that will appeal to preteen boys? A richly detailed historical novel about a character's internal journey? Identifying your goal can help you make decisions about what to cut and what to keep.

Next make a scene list, describing what each scene does.

• Do you need to make major changes to the plot, characters, setting, or theme (fiction) or the focus of the topic (nonfiction)?

• Does each scene fulfill the synopsis goal? How does it advance plot, reveal character, or both?

• Does each scene build and lead to the next? Are any redundant? If you cut the scene, would you lose anything? Can any secondary characters be combined or eliminated?

• Does anything need to be added or moved? Do you have a length limit or target?

• Can you increase the complications, so that at each step, more is at stake, there's greater risk or a better reward? If each scene has the same level of risk and consequence, the pacing is flat and the middle sags.

• Check for accuracy. Are your facts correct? Are your characters and setting consistent?

• Does each scene (in fiction) or paragraph (in nonfiction) follow a logical order and stick to the topic?

- Is your point of view consistent?
- Do you have dynamic language: Strong, active verbs? A variety of sentence lengths (but mostly short and to the point)? No clichés? Do you use multiple senses (sight, sound, taste, smell, touch)?
- Finally, edit for spelling and punctuation.

(For detailed editing questions, see my Plot Outline Exercise. It's in my book *Advanced Plotting* or available for download on my website: http://www.chriseboch.com/newsletter.htm)

Editing Description

For each detail, ask:
- Does it make the story more believable?
- Does it help readers picture or understand a character or place better?
- Does it answer questions that readers might want answered?
- Does it distract from the action?
- Could it be removed without confusing readers or weakening the story?
- For illustrated work, could the description be replaced by illustrations?

Use more details for unusual/unfamiliar settings. Try using multiple senses: sights, sounds, smells, tastes, and the feeling of touch. Especially in picture books, use senses other than sight, which can be shown through the illustrations.

Editing Resources:

Print/Ebook

Advanced Plotting, by Chris Eboch

Self-Editing for Fiction Writers, by Renni Browne and Dave King

Style That Sizzles & Pacing for Power – An Editor's Guide to Writing Compelling Fiction, by Jodie Renner

Manuscript Makeover, by Elizabeth Lyon

Novel Metamorphosis, by Darcy Pattison

Revision & Self-Editing, by James Scott Bell

Thanks, But This Isn't For Us, by Jessica Page Morrell

Online

I haven't tried this, but the "Hemingway App" is designed to identify overly long or complicated sentences, so it might be helpful in learning to simplify your work for younger audiences: www.hemingwayapp.com/

Grammarly is a free app that claims to find more errors than Microsoft Word's spelling and grammar check option, including words that are spelled correctly but used incorrectly: www.grammarly.com

Resources for Writers, by editor Jodie Renner, list several of her editing books as well as blog posts on various writing topics: http://jodierennerediting.blogspot.ca

The Plot Outline Exercise from *Advanced Plotting* helps you analyze your plot for trouble spots: http://www.krisbock.com/blog.htm

The Other Side of the Story blog, by middle grade author Janice Hardy, has great posts on many writing craft topics: http://blog.janicehardy.com

Author Jordan McCollum offers downloadable free writing guides on topics such as character arcs and deep point of view: http://jordanmccollum.com/free-writing-guides/

In "A Bad Case of Revisionitis," Literary agent Natalie M. Lakosil discusses when to stop revising: http://www.adventuresinagentland.com/2014/05/a-bad-case-of-revisionitis.html

Chapter 15: Critiques

If you are not writing for publication, and you don't care about improving as a writer, you don't need to take criticism from anyone. That's fine; it's totally your decision. But if you do hope to publish your work, or if you simply want to learn to be a better storyteller, you'll need to get feedback at some point. Few people are good at analyzing their own writing, so getting critiques is an important part of editing and learning how to improve your writing.

Getting critical feedback can be painful. Sometimes this comes from the critique partner being unnecessarily harsh. At other times, it comes from the writer being overly sensitive. If your manuscript is your "baby," you might not appreciate any comments that suggest it isn't perfect. But praise alone won't help you improve your writing.

Try to keep in mind that a critique isn't an insult. It's a way to help you make the manuscript even better. Also, it isn't about you as a person, or even you as a writer. It's about this particular manuscript, at this moment in time. If the manuscript is flawed, that's all right. In fact, it's usually a necessary part of the process. Most writers produce horrible, ugly, embarrassing manuscripts in the early stages. It's the editing that makes those stories wonderful. A quote contributed to several different authors is "You can't edit a blank page." Get something down, and then figure out how to make it better. Getting a critique can help you figure out how to make it better.

Finally, any critique advice is a matter of opinion. If several people are pointing out a problem, there's likely a problem. But if only one person makes a comment, and it doesn't resonate with you, it's fine to ignore it or get a second opinion. Ultimately you have to write something that pleases you; it's not your job to change your manuscript based on every piece of advice that anybody cares to give.

You can get feedback in several different ways. You can ask family and friends. You can join a critique group or otherwise network with other writers to exchange your manuscripts. You can take classes in person, online, or through the mail. Finally, you can hire a professional to provide a critique. Each of these options has pros and cons.

Family and Friends

You may have family members or friends who are happy to read your writing. Usually these people are not experienced writers. That means they may not know how to identify story problems or give advice about them. Still, they might be able to offer opinions from a reader's perspective. (Readers who are not necessarily writers are sometimes called "beta readers.")

When getting critiques from family and friends, it's best to keep your request simple. You might ask your readers to mark any place they:

- Are bored
- Are confused
- Don't believe things would happen that way

That's simple enough for anyone to follow, and it should point out trouble spots in the manuscript. For a little more detail, Freelance Editor Karen R. Sanderson offers this list to provide guidance to your critique partners:

Critical: Please provide an honest response, not only compliments.

Real: Does it feel real and does the dialogue read like people actually talk?

Imagery: Can you imagine the scenes, places, and people?

Timing: Did the timing of events, chapters, and character introductions make sense?

Interesting: Did it capture your interest or were you ready to put it down after the first paragraph?

Questions: Did you have questions? Were you unsure of what was happening or why?

Unique: Is it unique or is it like a dozen other books you wished you hadn't purchased?

Engaging: Were you engaged in the characters, the scenes, the events?

By giving a little direction, you emphasize that you truly want feedback (not only compliments), and you encourage people to look at the bigger picture and not just mark any typos they notice. Otherwise you may only hear good things. Praise is delightful, but when it comes from people you know, the rave reviews do not necessarily mean your work is wonderful. It could mean those people don't want to hurt your feelings. It could mean they don't read enough in this genre to tell good from bad. Or it could simply mean that they like you and are predisposed to enjoy anything you write.

The latter issue is especially common with reading stories to your children, grandchildren, or students. They enjoy the attention and it's fun to hear stories read aloud. People who know you well may also recognize family stories, which would not have the same appeal to an outside audience. For example, if you base a story on the antics of your family's cat, your children may love it, but it may not resonate the same way with strangers.

Many professionals warn against taking feedback from non-writers too seriously. Editors and agents do not want to hear in your query letter that your children, grandchildren, students, etc. loved your work. That's meaningless and might be taken as a sign that you are not a serious writer.

On the other hand, sometimes family members and friends offer blunt, even brutal, criticisms. Some people seem to think it's OK to be rude to a loved one in a way they wouldn't behave to a stranger. Some people may even be secretly trying to discourage you, so you'll spend more time on them and not your new hobby. Others may honestly be trying to help but not know how to give balanced, encouraging feedback. Or maybe they don't understand the kind of writing you are doing. Someone who only reads epic fantasy novels for adults may not be the best person to give feedback on a picture book for young children.

In short, feedback from friends and family can vary greatly in its helpfulness and hurtfulness. It can be especially crushing to hear negative reactions from a loved one. If someone's comments make you feel sad or discouraged, maybe you don't want to share your stories with that person in the future.

Of course, if you are not really ready to hear any criticism, don't ask for it. It's fine to share your work with family members or friends and let them know that you do not want comments, you simply want to share. If they insist on trying to provide criticism anyway, interrupt them. Make it clear that's not their job; you only want support.

Other Writers

Joining a critique group is often a great way to get feedback as well as emotional support for your journey as a writer. Reach out through local writing groups, writers' discussion boards, or Goodreads author groups. The Society of Children's Book Writers and Illustrators (SCBWI) "Blueboard" discussion boards have a section specifically for arranging manuscript critique exchanges. This section is available to SCBWI members only. Find the Blueboard here: http://www.scbwi.org/boards/index.php. You can also try putting up notices in libraries, bookstores, and cafes. (Be careful about listing personal information, and make sure you meet strangers in a public place.)

When you critique each other, try to keep in mind the "sandwich" method of giving feedback. You start by saying something you like about the manuscript. Then you offer some suggestions or ask questions. Finally, you end with more praise. When the more critical comments are sandwiched between compliments, it's easier to accept the advice. Note also that you should be offering *advice*, not *criticism*. What's the difference?

Your story is boring. – Criticism
I didn't notice a lot of conflict. Maybe if she had a stronger goal, with higher stakes, the story would be more dramatic. – Advice

Your character is a brat. I hated her. – Criticism
I couldn't really identify with your character. I wonder what about her appealed to you? Maybe if the reader understood her better, she'd be more likable. – Advice

Criticism points out a problem, often in a mean way. That tends to leave the writer discouraged and not wanting to write anymore. Advice points out problems in a gentler way, ideally with ideas for fixing the problem. Suggestions should be presented as options, not absolute truth. Advice acknowledges that this is only one reader's opinion; others may have a different reaction, and ultimately it's the writer's goal that matters. Good advice leaves the writer enthusiastic about working on the story.

Critique Group Challenges

Critique groups can be great. A good one can shorten your journey to publication by years. At their best, these groups are both a source of emotional support and a way to get thoughtful, detailed suggestions about your writing. If you have a supportive and helpful group, remember to say thank you (perhaps with hugs and chocolates).

Unfortunately, not every group is this wonderful. Some start well but fizzle out quickly, because not all members are committed. Others have trouble establishing a regular meeting time, although online groups can bring people together when they don't live in the same area. Beginning writers in particular may find it hard to join a serious, experienced critique group. Often the most accomplished writers want to work with other professionals, and established groups may be closed to new members. Still, you may be able to join or start a group with other beginning or intermediate writers. You can learn together and encourage each other. Some groups have started with all new writers and several years later had every member published.

In the worst case, a bad group, or even one bad person in a group, can be discouraging, even soul-crushing. Watch out for problems and act quickly to protect yourself. This could mean leaving the group, starting a splinter group with some members, or setting up new rules for the current members.

Individual writers have different levels of sensitivity. If you find any critical comment horrifying, the problem may lie with you, and you'll need to either develop thicker skin, or write for your own enjoyment but not expect anyone else to publish or review your work.

On the other hand, if you're normally open to suggestions but a particular critique partner leaves you feeling like you never want to write again, you may need to end that relationship. If you have a good group except for one problem person, you might discuss the issue with other members of the group. Do you think the person might respond to a direct request for a change in behavior? If not, maybe that person could be politely informed that they are not a good fit for the group. Or you could disband the group and start a new one without telling them. If you don't take some action, the group will fall apart and you'll lose everyone.

Critique Group Characters

Watch out for the following personality types in a critique group:

- The Cheerleader. She loves everything you do! This is gratifying, especially when you are doubting your talent, but it's not particularly helpful in improving your work.
- The Grammarian. He doesn't have a lot to say about the content of your work, but he'll circle every typo in red pen and may insist you follow strict grammar rules that have gone out of date. (By the way, I *never* use red pen on critiques – blue, purple, or green ink stands out from the black text, without that negative association of graded English papers.)
- The Mouse. You can't tell whether or not she likes your work, because she never voices an opinion. She might hide behind the excuse that she's not experienced enough to offer feedback. She'll do this for years.
- The Perpetual Beginner. He truly isn't experienced enough to offer feedback, and he never seems to improve. This type can be divided into The Rut, who brings in the same manuscript over and over without ever making substantial changes (despite all your thoughtful advice) and The Hummingbird, who throws away a manuscript as soon as it's gotten one negative comment, preferring to work on something new.
- The Chatterbox. She wants to talk about anything and everything – other than the manuscripts you're supposed to be critiquing. This person sees a writing group as a social occasion, not a way to improve your craft.
- Father Knows Best. He always has an opinion, which he voices clearly and often. He prefers to discuss how he would write the story if it were his own, ignoring the author's vision.
- The Bully. She enjoys tearing apart your manuscript. No suggestions, just criticisms bordering on insults.

All these characters have one thing in common. They don't help you improve your work. Having one Cheerleader in the group can be nice, as it means you'll hear some praise. The Grammarian may be useful, although often those comments are unnecessary and time-consuming when you are still developing a story and focusing on the big picture, not proofreading.

The Mouse and the Perpetual Beginner don't do a lot of harm, but they waste your time. Why should you spend hours doing thoughtful critiques when you're not getting anything in return? (Note, sometimes these people can learn over time. Ask for the specific feedback you want or encourage them to use one of the lists of critiques provided in this chapter. But if they won't make an effort to be better critique partners, it may be time to end the relationship.)

The Chatterbox is an even bigger time waster. Sometimes that person can be controlled by having a set time for visiting, perhaps the first or last half hour of each meeting. Including some social time is a way for the group to bond. Some critique groups like to start or end with a nice potluck meal. You could also have one or two meetings a year that are purely social. If there's a way to get Father Knows Best or the Bully to change their behavior, I don't know it. They should be avoided.

A good critique is kind and supportive, pointing out both good qualities and weak spots in your manuscript, and giving you ideas for how to improve it. The best critiques leave you fired up and ready to get to work on revisions, even if you know you have a lot of work ahead. Look for people who can provide that.

Taking Classes

Do a little searching, and chances are you'll find many options for writing classes to suit every need. Often community colleges offer classes. So do some senior centers or community centers. Writing organizations often have meetings that may include short workshops. They may also sponsor classes or conferences. The Society of Children's Book Writers and Illustrators is an international organization with regional branches around the world. See if they have meetings in your area.

You might find paid classes, free meetings, or social events through other local groups, such as Sisters in Crime, Romance Writers of America, or Science Fiction & Fantasy Writers of America. While these groups don't focus on writing for children, you could learn valuable writing techniques. There are also local or regional groups, such as SouthWest Writers, based in Albuquerque, New Mexico. The Writing Barn in Austin, Texas, has picture book classes and other writing events, some paid and some free.

If you can't find a local class at a convenient time and place, you still have options. Several organizations and individuals offer classes online or through the mail. Two well-known organizations focusing on writing for kids are The Institute of Children's Literature and Children's Book Insider.

You'll find a lot of variety in costs, course material, and how much feedback is provided. Shop around to find the class that works best for you. Do you want to learn the business side of publishing or focus on craft techniques? Do you want lectures with no homework? Do you want specific feedback from an expert teacher on your own work? Make sure that is included.

As an example, Gotham Writers Workshop offers a ten-week children's book writing class for $400 (as of this writing). This fee covers lectures, writing exercises, and two opportunities for critiques. The Picture Book Academy offers a five-week course focused on picture books for $379. It includes access to a critique group and help through conference calls; a personal critique with a teacher is an extra $100. The Online Writing Workshops by author Anastasia Suen cost $299 and involves 12 lessons, with several critiques. She has workshops that focus on children's novels, picture book biographies, nonfiction picture books, and rhyming picture books.

These are only a few of the many options. They are listed as examples or what's available; I'm not offering a personal recommendation. Many experienced authors give workshops in person or online, so check out local events or browse online offerings. You can sign up for my mailing list to learn about my upcoming webinars here: http://eepurl.com/040_j

You'll also find some wonderful writing retreats available, some for a weekend and some for a week or more. Many are put on by SCBWI, in lovely locations around the world. The Highlights Foundation has regular retreats in Honesdale, Pennsylvania, on a variety of subjects related to writing for children. They are highly praised for the content, the setting, and the food. While the retreats are expensive, Highlights gives many scholarships.

Some retreats may have a particular focus. For example, Picture Book Boot Camp in western Massachusetts, run by authors Jane Yolen and Heidi Stemple, is a master class for picture book authors. Other retreats cover all genres or simply allow writers time to work on their own projects.

One bonus to taking a class or attending a retreat is that you may meet other writers, who could become your critique partners after the class ends. This is easier with a live class, but even an online class may offer a chance for students to chat and connect.

Hiring a Pro

It's tempting to stick with trading manuscripts for free, and you may get some excellent feedback that way. However, getting feedback from family, friends, and even other writers might not be enough to perfect your work. Many critique partners won't want to read your manuscript through multiple revisions. And unless they are experienced writers and writing teachers, critique partners may miss issues a professional editor would catch.

Hiring a pro may provide better advice. You might ask a friend to help you bandage a scraped knee, but if you have a bone sticking out of your leg, you're going to the hospital. When the situation is serious, professional experience counts, so if you are serious about your writing, consider using a professional editor.

Professional developmental editors can help writers shape their manuscripts. They can help beginning or intermediate writers identify weak spots in their skill sets, acting as a one-on-one tutor. They provide expertise that family and friends, and even critique partners, often lack. A professional editor will prioritize your work because it's a job.

Some of my critique clients have mentioned that they've taken a manuscript through a critique group, but they know it still needs work. They've gone as far as they can with critique group help, so they're turning to a paid critique. If someone is paying me several hundred dollars to critique a novel, I'm going to devote my time to getting it done well and quickly. I'll dig deep and be as tough – but helpful – as I can be. My novel critique letters typically run five or six single-spaced pages, with comments broken down into categories such as Characters, Setting, Plot (Beginning, Middle, and End), Theme, and Style. Most critique group members don't have that kind of time, even if they have the skills to identify the problems.

If you aren't sure if you need professional help, do a trial run with a manuscript you've finished. Send out a half dozen queries to agents or editors and see what kind of response you get. I've had clients come to me because editors have turned down a manuscript they "didn't love enough." This is a good indicator that the idea may be strong, but the writing isn't there yet. No hired editor can guarantee that your manuscript will ever sell, but a good editor can improve the manuscript and also teach you to be a better writer.

Again, if you are writing purely for your own enjoyment, or to share your work with family and friends, you don't need to worry about producing something of publishable quality. But if you are writing for publication, and agents or editors don't seem impressed with your work, a professional critique can teach you a lot.

Even if you decide to hire a freelancer, you'll get more from the experience by turning in a draft you've already edited. According to freelance editor Linda Lane, "Carefully preparing your manuscript for an editor rather than simply forwarding the latest draft saves dollars, because freelance editors often charge an hourly rate."

Use the tips in Chapter 14: Editing to revise your manuscript as much as you can on your own. If you have critique partners, revise based on their feedback as well. Then start looking for a professional editor. However, if you want a professional critique on the content of your book – the plot, characters, overall writing style, and so forth – don't wait until you think you have a completely polished draft. If it turns out you have major problems with the plot or character development, it's better to identify those before you've gone through 10 drafts and have proofread the whole thing.

Ask other writers for recommendations to editors. Try the SCBWI online discussion boards or local writers' groups. Make sure the editor has experience with the kind of writing you are doing. Someone who only writes for adults is probably not the best editor for your children's picture book.

Communicate clearly with a prospective editor to make sure you know what you're getting. Typically content or developmental editors look at the big picture items. Copy editors and proofreaders can catch inconsistencies and spelling or grammar errors. Start by working with someone who will focus on content, structure, and stylistic weaknesses. Don't pay someone to fix your typos when you might still have major changes to make. Ask questions or ask for a sample to make sure you are hiring the right editor for your needs.

Finally, just because a professional tells you something doesn't mean they're right, or that you need to do what they say. Two qualified professionals may have different opinions on a subject. It's *your* story, so do what you feel will make the story better.

This is a long chapter, because getting critiques, and learning from them, is a big part of learning to write well. Depending on your needs and goals, hopefully some of the ideas in this section will work for you.

Professional Editors

A list of past and present instructors from the Institute of Children's Literature who critique for a fee: http://www.institutechildrenslit.com/rx/ws01/instructors.shtml

Advanced Critique Questions

Critiquing is an advanced skill, and it can take time to learn how to do it well. The following questions can help you give a better critique. You can also use them with critique partners, asking for specific feedback. This is a long list, so it might be too much to expect critique partners to answer every question. If you think that's the case, pick out the questions most important to you at this time. (You can download a Word version of this list to print and reuse at the "For Writers" tab on my website, at http://www.chriseboch.com/newsletter.htm)

1. Does the opening hook you?

2. Is the setting clear and specific? Is it carried throughout the story? Are the five senses used? Is there good use of imagery?

3. Is the main character believable, distinct, well-rounded, and interesting? Does she or he have both weaknesses and strengths? Is the internal conflict carried throughout the story? Are the character's motives clear?

4. Does the hero solve his or her own problems?

5. Is the villain realistic, with both weaknesses and strengths? Is he/she/it a serious challenge?

6. Are secondary characters believable, distinct, well-rounded, and interesting? Do they have both weaknesses and strengths?

7. Is the point of view clear and consistent? Does the reader feel close to the story or distant? Does this work?

8. Is there a good balance between narrative description, action, and dialogue? Are there summarized passages that should be written out as scenes? Vice versa?

9. Is the dialogue natural and convincing? Does each character speak in a unique, consistent, appropriate voice? Does the dialogue move the story forward and/or add to character development?

10. Is the plot believable? Is it interesting? Do you think there are any weaknesses? Is the conflict clear? Does it build to a climax? Is the ending satisfying? Do the characters behave throughout in realistic ways?

11. Does the story start and end in the right place? Should it start or end sooner or later?

12. Is the important action written out as scenes (shown on stage)? Is every scene necessary to move the plot forward? Does each chapter or scene have an opening hook and a final cliffhanger? Is the pacing effective, with good scene transitions (for example, are jumps in time, flashbacks, etc. clear)? Do emotional or humorous scenes evoke the right response?

13. What is the theme? Is it unclear, or too obvious? Is it carried throughout the piece? Is it appropriate for the audience?

14. Is the style fresh and unique, free of clichés? Is the language appropriate for the audience? Does the tone fit the subject? Is there a variety of sentence lengths and styles?

15. Does it need to be trimmed and tightened?

16. Did you notice any technical errors – spelling, punctuation, grammar, etc.?

17. What are the story's major strengths?

18. What are the story's major weaknesses?

19. Suggest ways to improve the story.

Chapter 16:
Writing for the Right Age

Writing for children is different from writing for adults in a few important ways. One issue is the need to consider reading level. The grade level or reading level needs to fit the audience. For example, kindergartners might be able to understand a story if they heard it read aloud, when they wouldn't actually be able to read it. A first-grader who is learning to read may have trouble with more advanced grammar, such as contractions and compound sentences. Most fifth-graders cannot read material written at a high school level. This means a story aimed at elementary children can look quite different from one aimed at teenagers.

If you are using Microsoft Word, you can get an idea of the grade level of your work. It's simply a matter of having grammar check turned on along with spell check. Search for "readability" in the Help menu for instructions. You can check a complete story or article, a paragraph, or even a single sentence. This is a great way to explore how changing your wording changes your reading level. Write a paragraph and check the grade level. Then edit the paragraph and check the grade level again. In general, simpler vocabulary and shorter sentences will make the reading level lower. Play with the language to see if you can simplify it even more. Do this over and over, and see how things change.

Let's try an example. Here's a made-up sentence for an imaginary fantasy story:

She barreled down the lengthy hallway, staggering to a stop in the rotunda, where an enormous mythical creature was ascending from a gaping chasm.

A lot is wrong with that sentence, including too much action packed into two lines. The main point for this example is that it comes out at a 12.9 reading level. (That's means it's appropriate for the ninth month of 12th grade.) Let's try to simplify it. First, I'll simply break it into two sentences:

She barreled down the lengthy hallway and staggered to a stop in the rotunda. An enormous mythical creature was ascending from a gaping chasm.

That brought it down to an 7.7 grade level. The first sentence is at a 6.7 reading level, and the second sentence is at 9.5. That's fine for a young adult novel, and probably all right for a middle grade novel, so long as the entire book isn't written at such a high level. But what if the target audience is younger? Let's try some more changes.

She barreled down the long hallway. In a large, circular hall, she staggered to a stop. A giant mythical creature was rising from a gaping crack in the ground.

Overall, that's now at a 4.4 reading level. The first two sentences are easy enough for early middle grade, or even upper elementary. In the last sentence, replacing *enormous*, *ascending*, and *chasm* with simpler words brought it down to a 6.7 grade level. It's a few words longer than the previous version, but *crack in the ground* is easier than *chasm*. I tried replacing *mythical* with *fairytale*, but that didn't change the grade level. Replacing *creature* with *animal* made it worse. Of course, maybe I could figure out what kind of mythical creature it is, and name it or describe it in simple detail. That would not only get rid of the challenging words, but would also create a clearer picture. Worrying about reading level might sound restrictive, but in reality, simpler writing is often clearer, and therefore more effective.

You don't need to mention the grade level when you submit work, unless the publisher specifically asks for it. Publishers don't usually care about the computerized grade level, unless books are targeted at the school and library market. Still, checking your grade level is a good way to get an idea of the complexity of your work. If you are trying to write stories for elementary school children, but your writing is coming out at a high school grade level, you have a problem.

Writing for the Right Age

You can either learn to write at a lower reading level, or target your work to high school students. Or you could do some of each!

Of course, regardless of your readership age, you want your stories and articles to be fun and engaging. This usually means straightforward language and relatively simple sentences. Forget the dry, academic language you may have learned in college or on the job. Look for lively, active verbs, language that paints a clear picture, and a good mix of action and dialogue, with just enough description to set the scene. In addition, try to keep your sentences short and simple, but with enough variety that the story does not sound clunky. Reading the work aloud is a good way to check this.

Another great exercise is retyping a published story, article, picture book, or a few pages of a novel. By typing the words yourself, you get a feel for appropriate language for that audience. For a picture book, you also get to see how the story would look in manuscript format, without illustrations and page breaks.

You can also use the *Children's Writer's Word Book* to check which words are at what reading level, and to find suggestions for alternatives.

There's another advantage to keeping your writing relatively simple. One of the keys to writing well for children is writing "tight," with no unnecessary words. Most magazines have a limit on the length of story or article they will accept, and often the word count can't be very high. You need to pack a lot into a small space. Picture books are also often less than 500 words. You'll have more flexibility with novels, but the pacing should still feel fast. Tight writing is typically more interesting and fun to read. Try to say things in the fewest words possible, as long as you can still be clear and interesting. That will keep your story moving, and often help your grade level suit the audience as well.

Tips for Tapping into Your Younger Self

Not everyone finds it easy to remember the truth of being a child, or to express those feelings in a childlike manner. If your writing winds up sounding too adult, or if you struggle to figure out how a child or teenager would think and act, try these exercises. Some can also be helpful for getting in touch with today's children, whose experiences may be different from when we were young.

• Try writing by hand rather than directly on the computer. Some people recommend using your non-dominant hand. Perhaps use a large sheet of paper and crayons. You can even interview your child-self. When you ask questions, write with your dominant hand (if you are right-handed, that is your dominant hand). Switch to your other hand to answer. (If you had a traumatic childhood, this exercise may uncover traumatic memories. Be prepared to offer love to your child-self and your adult-self. An Internet search for "healing your inner child" will provide more advice and resources.)

• Study EMDR (Eye Movement Desensitization and Reprocessing). This technique was developed as a treatment for trauma, but it has also been used by artists and actors to improve performance. Try *Emotional Healing at Warp Speed: The Power of EMDR*, by David Grand, for an overview and a self-use chapter that includes using a technique for increased creativity. Another self-help guide for the layperson is *Getting Past Your Past: Take Control of Your Life with Self-Help Techniques from EMDR Therapy*, by Francine Shapiro.

• Look over photos from your childhood. Try to remember what was happening in your life at that time. Perhaps tell stories out loud about those days, even if the only one listening is your pet.

• If you kept journals or a diary as a child or teenager, and you still have them, review them. Don't judge either the quality of the writing or the feelings. Allow yourself to connect with that young person and feel the strength of their emotions again. Stories and artwork you created as a child can bring back memories as well.

• Use the questions under "Finding the Seeds of Stories" in Chapter 2: Finding Ideas, as writing prompts. You can do a fun twist on this idea with a writing partner. You each tell a brief story about a childhood experience that was exciting, scary, or whatever. Then you write the other person's story, making up details to fit. This option may make it easier to concentrate on telling a great story rather than on being historically accurate.

- Volunteer at a school, summer camp, house of worship children's program, or anywhere else where you can spend time with kids. You can also offer to babysit or take out friends' kids for the day. Pay attention to what interests them, how they move, and how they talk. What reminds you of your own childhood? What is different?

- Hang out where kids hang out — the mall food court, a playground, the city pool — and observe and take notes. As long as you are discreet, chances are no one will notice what you are doing. However, if you're concerned that people will find your behavior creepy, bring along this writing guide to point out the exercise to anyone who questions you. (I've never heard of anyone being questioned, despite thousands of students who have done this exercise through the Institute of Children's Literature. Obviously you shouldn't follow or a approach a child you don't know. Observing from a distance is fine.)

- You can also try meeting with a few writing partners to observe children. Sometimes illustrators will get together at a public place with lots of kids, such as the zoo, to do sketches. Writers can do the same, making word sketches. Spend ten or fifteen minutes writing, and then share your work aloud.

- Play. As your body permits, try hopscotch, jacks, skipping, jumping rope, or whatever games you played as a child. Play on a playground: climb the monkey bars, swing, go down the slide, take a spin on the merry-go-round. Ask the kids you know to teach you their games, whether computer-based, on paper, or physical. Play with action figures or dolls. Try a coloring book, sticker book, paper dolls, or other interactive kids' book.

- *Feeling Like a Kid*, by Jerry Griswold, explores how children think and shows how great children's literature understands what it's like to be a child.

Chapter 17:
Writing a Successful Picture Book

Selling a picture book is challenging. Yet even when the market is at its weakest, a few picture books find many thousands of devoted readers: witness success stories such as *Olivia*, by Ian Falconer; *Fancy Nancy*, by Jane O'Connor, illustrated by Robin Preiss Glasser; *Don't Let the Pigeon Drive the Bus*, by Mo Willems; and *Skippyjon Jones*, by Judy Schachner. These books not only had enormous sales, they also spawned equally popular sequels. They became that holy grail of picture book publishing, a franchise: a series that can go on for multiple best-selling books.

These books have one important thing in common: they are character-driven. When remembering these books, we think less of what happened, and more of what the character is like. *Fancy Nancy* is about a girl who likes everything highly decorated. *Skippyjon Jones* is about an imaginative Siamese kitten who pretends to be a Chihuahua. The plot comes from the character's personality, not external events.

Jamie Weiss Chilton, an agent with the Andrea Brown Literary Agency, Inc., says, "A character-driven picture book is one in which the character is meant to be the story's main focus, a story in which we care about the action *because* we care about the character."

Character is so important that "everything that occurs in the story happens because of the personality, decisions, and actions of the main character," explains Liz Waniewski, Editor, Dial Books for Young Readers. "The character is the driving force behind events in the story; things don't happen to the character, things happen because of the character."

Susan Kochan, Associate Editorial Director at G.P. Putnam's Sons, adds an example. "To me, a character-driven picture book is one where the unique qualities of a character make him or her face a problem or challenge in a new distinct way that stands out from other treatments. *Stand Tall, Molly Lou Melon* (by Patty Lovell) is about a girl facing a bully in her new school. That story has been done many times, but Molly Lou stands up to Ronald Durkin by putting all the great advice her grandmother has given her into practice. Her confidence and creativity are shown through quirky actions that kids love – stacking pennies on her buck teeth instead of being embarrassed, running under Ronald Durkin's legs during a football game shows that being short isn't all bad. From these clever actions, readers know they're meeting someone fun and new and special."

"Pluck would be a key quality," says Caitlyn M. Dlouhy, Editorial Director at Atheneum Books for Young Children. "Look at our more modern-day characters: Pigeon, Olivia, Ladybug Girl [by David Soman and Jacky Davis], Duck [from *Click, Clack, Moo: Cows That Type* by Doreen Cronin and Betsy Lewin] to name a few. They all have a strong sense of who they are (or who they want to be), and all have gumption. Then, if you look back to our 'classics', there's Madeleine and Eloise and Cat (of Hat fame) and Winnie the Pooh, and they, too, all have that sense of pluck."

But don't think you can get away without a strong plot. "A character-driven picture book is more than just a dimensional, unique character," notes Laurent Linn, Art Director at Simon & Schuster Books For Young Readers. "There has to be the full story arc of beginning, middle, and end, just as you would find in a plot-driven book." Character may come first, but don't let that character wander around aimlessly. Even the most interesting person needs a goal and obstacles to truly shine.

Just Like Me (Or How I Want to Be)

The best characters become quirky friends to the reader. "If you ask most any kid (or any adult, for that matter) to name some favorite picture books, chances are many of the answers will not be the name of actual picture books, but of characters," says Dlouhy.

The reader feels a connection with that character, a bond that goes beyond a single book. Identifying with that character allows a child to step out of the confines of his or her own restricted world. "A young child's world is very narrow, actually, and the world revolves around his or her self," says Linn. "So stepping into a character's shoes isn't just about identifying with a character, but going on a journey as well – discovering new places, new people, and new ways of experiencing the universe."

Perhaps this is why, as Kochan says, "The successful ones star clever, funny characters. Fancy Nancy is flamboyant in the way lots of little girls want to be (if their parents would let them). Skippyjon Jones has a can-do attitude that all of us should aspire to. Once kids find a character they can laugh at, they are attached and will follow that character through other adventures."

Dlouhy adds, "Kids can explore their worlds through the eyes of great characters, experience or share emotions, recognize themselves in some characters, giggle at crazy foibles, have adventures they could never quite have in day to day life."

Editors recognize the value of that relatability. "I want this type of story because the main character is who I relate to when reading any book," Waniewski says. "It makes it easier and more fun for a reader to put herself into that character's shoes and be part of the story. I think this is the reason they are so successful, too — a character-driven story gives readers something to relate to immediately. We probably all know someone like Olivia, Fancy Nancy, Ladybug Girl, Skippyjon Jones, or the Pigeon."

If the character's personality dominates the first book, it's relatively easy to put that character in a new situation and let the strong personality shine through. As Weiss Chilton notes, "A character-driven picture book easily leads to sequels and a brand." Readers recognize an old friend and are excited to see how he or she tackles a new challenge. Because these books are so much about the character, they can give a fresh feel to an old topic, such as the first day of school or not wanting to go to bed. Weiss Chilton says, "I love to see a completely fresh take on a tried and true theme."

Developing a character that can carry a franchise isn't easy, though. "Realistically, it's a very rare thing," Linn says. "It's not a defined science or we'd all have character franchises. But, if we look at what makes some of these characters in children's literature so successful, I think it's what makes any character successful: depth, uniqueness, humor, adventure, tenacity, hope, capacity for growth and change, and a big heart."

That doesn't mean you can just imitate successful existing characters, however. "They have to have a unique personality that makes them different from the other franchise characters out there, and still have enough broadness of personality to have many different kinds of adventures," Waniewski says. "All the adventures do have to relate in some way to their distinct personalities."

The Artist's Advantage

"Illustrators who also write have a bit of a leg up in this genre because they can say a lot through expressions and body language right from the start," Kochan says. "I think that's why some of the successful franchises are by author/illustrators."

She mentions the Llama, Llama books by Anna Dewdney, Strega Nona by Tomie dePaola, Skippyjon Jones, and Olivia as examples. Try reading just the text of Olivia, and the story doesn't seem that special. It's the illustrations that show what's really going on in Olivia's world, and mind.

If you're not an illustrator, you have to work even harder on developing the character through their action and dialogue. You'll also need to consider visual opportunities for the story. "Most preschool kids can't read yet, so the illustrations are their only way of interpreting the story unfiltered," Linn points out. "Thinking visually as one writes a story is essential, even if the writer isn't an artist at all."

As an Art Director, Linn says, "I look for text that suggests a variety of possibilities for an illustrator to take and run with. As a very general (and not always possible) rule, whatever is written in the text shouldn't be in the art, and whatever is in the art shouldn't be in the text. The writer should, with spare words, be able to hint at visual images without describing them. Very hard to do, but magic when it's done just right."

Could You Be Next?

Many authors focus more on the concept or plot when developing a picture book, and then develop a character to fit the situation. A strong plot, or a fresh take on a standard concept, can certainly help a writer develop a picture book idea. But spending additional time on character development might create a stronger book – and increase the opportunities for sequels.

To get started developing strong picture book characters, "Read, read, read!" Linn says. "See what has or hasn't worked before. Look at the best of the best, classics and new, as well as books that aren't so well known. A good children's librarian will help guide you."

Weiss Chilton advises, "As a writing exercise, give your character a whole back story – a background that includes lots of details about them that won't be seen in the story. It will help you as the author have a better sense of your character and that development will come through in your writing."

And finally, don't get too caught up in the idea of franchise potential. "Don't get ahead of yourself," Linn says. "Meaning, focus on just one book with just one story. You may hope that your book and character will take off and a series will follow. But, it all starts with that one book."

Books mentioned:

Olivia, by Ian Falconer (Atheneum/Anne Schwartz Books)
Fancy Nancy, by Jane O'Connor, illustrated by Robin Preiss Glasser (HarperCollins)
Don't Let the Pigeon Drive the Bus, by Mo Willems (Hyperion Press)
Skippyjon Jones, by Judy Schachner (Puffin)
Ladybug Girl, by David Soman and Jacky Davis (Dial)
Stand Tall, Molly Lou Melon by Patty Lovell (Putnam Juvenile)
Click, Clack, Moo: Cows That Type by Doreen Cronin and Betsy Lewin (Simon & Schuster Children's Publishing)
Llama Llama Red Pajama by Anna Dewdney (Viking Juvenile)

A Note on Illustrations

You do not need to provide illustrations for your picture book when you submit it to a publisher. The publisher will want to choose an illustrator. They may have ideas about the best style for this book. They might want to pair a beginning author with a well-known illustrator. They will definitely want to work with you on editing the manuscript before the illustrator ever starts her or his job. If you get a family member or friend to do illustrations for you, you'll look like an amateur and hurt your chances of selling the manuscript. If you'd love to work with an illustrator you know, wait until you have an offer on the book, and then ask the editor to consider that artist's work.

If you are a professional illustrator, and you want to illustrate your own books, that's a different situation. But keep in mind, it's possible a publisher will like the story but not the illustrations. Make sure that both your writing and your artwork are top-notch publishable quality. Rather than illustrating the whole book before submitting, send the manuscript with about three sample illustrations. That way you can work as a team on polishing the story before committing to every image. You could also submit only the manuscript, and if you get a publisher's interests, ask them to look at your artwork.

If you want to self-publish, then you will need to arrange for illustrations on your own. If this is a family project, for your own enjoyment, you might pair with a family member or friend you know. However, if you hope to attract a broader audience, you should try to work with a professional children's book illustrator. Not an amateur, and not even somebody who is a talented artist with no experience in illustrating children's books. Illustrating picture books is a special skill. Illustrators have to think about page layout and text placement. They should produce a variety of illustrations, some close-up and some more distant, with characters in different active, engaging poses. The illustrations should tell a story on their own, adding to the text, not simply copying the words in a visual form. They also need to know how to save the art as the right kind of digital files to send to the printer.

Becoming a professional children's book illustrator takes years of training! If you are self-publishing and need to hire an illustrator, expect to pay for their professional services. There really isn't a standard rate, as it depends on the experience level of the illustrator, the complexity of their illustration style (in other words, how long it takes to complete an illustration), and the scope of the project. How many illustrations will they be doing? Are they doing text layout, end pages and overall design as well?

If you want a standard 16-page book of full-color illustrations, you should expect to pay at least a few thousand dollars. Professional illustrators typically get $2,000-$20,000 per book, plus royalties. Sign a contract that states who owns the rights to the images. Perhaps the illustrator owns the copyright, but you have the right to use the artwork for marketing as well as in the book.

For more information on working with an illustrator for self-publishing, see this article by artist and writer Dani Jones: http://tinyurl.com/ofgz4b6

A Note on Rhyme

Blame it on Dr. Seuss: Many beginning picture book writers try to write in rhyme. Not that rhyme is a bad thing, but *bad* rhyme is a bad thing. And there's far too much bad rhyme being written and sent to publishers. You may even hear editors and agents say they don't want to see stories in rhyme. They're tired of all the rotten rhyme.

Yet many rhyming picture books are published every year. Editors, parents, and children love a great rhyming picture book. Unfortunately, most beginners are not able to write rhyme really well. If you are not a talented poet, you might be better off writing your story in prose. You'll find plenty of great non-rhyming stories published as well.

If you want to write in rhyme, make sure you understand poetry. Do you know the terms rhythm, meter, and perfect rhyme — and can you use those techniques? Can you keep your language natural? Don't have children use old-fashioned words they would never use in real life. Don't twist sentences into weird grammatical orders in order to keep the rhyming word at the end. And avoid overly-simple, singsong, common rhymes such as *sun, done, one, begun.*

It's also a good idea to start with a draft that isn't in rhyme. Or if the story "comes to you" in rhyme, you should still do a draft that doesn't rhyme. Focus on the story — developing a great character, introducing a conflict early, adding complications, and having the main character solve the problem in the end. I often see beginner manuscripts where the story goes off in random directions, because the writer is focused on finding a good rhyme rather than telling a good story.

Rhyme can add to a great story, but it can't save a bad one. The story must always come first.

Poetry beyond Picture Books

While we're on the topic of poetry, many children's magazines use poems. That could be a good market if you love writing poetry. Poetry collections are also sometimes published as books. These usually collect poems around a specific theme, such as a season, school, or animals. One example is *What's for Dinner?: Quirky, Squirmy Poems from the Animal World*, by Katherine B. Hauth, illustrated by David Clark.

By the way, even books for older readers can use poetry. Verse novels may use a specific type of poetry, such as sonnets, or they may mix types of poems. Most are in free verse, not rhyme. Some examples of novels in verse are *Heartbeat*, by Sharon Creech, and *Out of the Dust*, by Karen Hesse. Ellen Hopkins is well-known for her edgy, young adult novels, which tackle tough subjects such as drug addiction (*Crank*) and teen prostitution (*Tricks*), using a series of poems. *A Wreath for Emmett Till* by Marilyn Nelson, illustrated by Philippe Lardy, is an unusual nonfiction example. The book uses a poetic form known as a "heroic crown of sonnets" to tell the story of a 14-year-old black boy murdered in 1955.

Caroline Starr Rose is the author of two historical verse novels. *May B.*, set in the 1870s in Kansas, is about a girl abandoned in a tiny sod house as winter approaches. *Blue Birds*, set in 1587 on the island of Roanoke, tells a story of friendship between two girls, one an English settler and one a native girl. Caroline notes that in novels, "Poems should be able stand alone. Each poem in a verse novel must capture one moment, scene, idea, mark of change in your character's life. Poems should also be able to function separately from the rest of the story."

At the same time, she says, "Poems must contribute to the whole. When I worked through *May B.*, I kept a quilt in mind, treating each poem like its own square of fabric. Each patch had to be able to function separately while at the same time move the story forward. Verse novels aren't books with strange line breaks. They are stories best communicated through the language, rhythm, imagery and structure of poetry."

Exercise:

Try making a picture book "dummy" from your manuscript. A dummy is a mock-up of your book. It could be several small sketches on a single page. Or you can simply staple a bunch of regular-sized pieces of paper together, one for each page in the finished book, and put text and illustrations on each page.

This is not something you will send to a publisher (unless you are also an illustrator). Rather, it is for your own use, so you can see how your words would look laid out in picture book format. Do you have some pages with a lot of text, and some with almost none? Does that work, or would it be better to spread out the text more evenly? Do you have a lot of text on one page because you are including description that could be covered by the illustrations? Are you explaining too much, or giving a lot of character thoughts, instead of focusing on action and dialogue?

You can also check the illustration potential. Don't worry about making great artwork; stick figures are fine. The idea is to make sure you have a variety of interesting images on each page. You might find, for example, that your adorable story about a kitten looking for a place to sleep means you'll have a lot of illustrations of a kitten sleeping. Is that enough variety for an engaging picture book? If not, how can you edit the manuscript? Or would it be better as a magazine story? (See the next chapter on "Picture Book Versus Short Story.")

Do an Internet search for "How to Make a Picture Book Dummy" and you'll find many instructions and examples.

Exercise:

Try this one with a critique group or a few friends interested in picture books. Each of you choose three books from the library or your personal stash. Try to find books that the others in the group might not know well. Look for books with a separate author and illustrator. (Books with a combined author-illustrator often depend more on the illustrations than the text.)

Each of you should type up the text from the books you've chosen in manuscript format. Make enough copies so everyone in the group has one.

Get together and critique the manuscripts. How do they work with only the text? What is the balance of action, dialogue, and description? Is the story engaging? Can you imagine the illustrations?

Then share the published book. What do the illustrations add to the story? Did the illustrator go beyond what was suggested in the text?

This exercise is designed to help you understand the difference between a text-only manuscript and a finished book. How can you use what you learned in your own manuscripts?

Picture Book Resources

Writing Picture Books: A Hands-On Guide from Story Creation to Publication, by Ann Whitford Paul, is a well-reviewed guide focusing on writing picture books.

Writing with Pictures: How to Write and Illustrate Children's Books, by Uri Shulevitz, is an older book, but especially good if you want to illustrate as well as write.

How to Write a Children's Picture Book, and *30 Days to a Stronger Picture Book*, by Darcy Pattison, share insight from a popular writing teacher. Darcy also blogs about picture books: http://www.darcypattison.com/category/picture-books/

Story Skeletons: Teaching Plot Structure with Picture Books discusses different kinds of plots with examples of picture books that use them: http://www.readingrockets.org/article/22242

The Three Commandments of Writing a Picture Book, from Write for Kids, offers some good, quick rules: http://writeforkids.org/2014/08/the-three-commandments-of-writing-a-picture-book/

At Writing Picture Books for Children, picture book author Patrice Sherman shares tips on writing picture books, including types of picture books and manuscript formatting: http://www.writingpicturebooksforchildren.com/

Writing Stories in Rhythm and Rhyme, by Dori Chaconas: http://www.dorichaconas.com/Icing%20the%20Cake%20page.htm

The Beat Goes On — Or, How To Be A Meter Reader: Identifying Rhythm Troublespots In Your Rhyming Picture Book Story, by Debbie Diesen, also covers poetry: http://www.juliehedlund.com/debbie-diesen-may-12-x-12-featured-author/

Chapter 18:
Picture Book Versus Short Story

Many children's literature writers want to write picture books. However, a lot of the "picture book" manuscripts I see would be better off as short stories. Sometimes that's due to the subject. For a picture book to be successful, it must sell at least 20,000 copies at $16 or more. That means each story has to have broad appeal to the parents, grandparents, and librarians who buy those books. It has to be a book they can imagine reading to their children dozens, if not hundreds, of times.

Magazines, on the other hand, usually have a mix of fiction and nonfiction on a variety of topics, perhaps with poetry and crafts. Each individual piece does not need to attract such a wide audience. A biography of a little-known person might not have wide enough appeal as a picture book. A sweet bedtime story might struggle to stand out against the dozens of similar books already on the market. Either of these might do very well in a magazine.

It's also important to remember that picture books are typically targeted at younger children, up to about age 5 or 6. Some picture books are for elementary school children and may be used in the classroom, but these are often nonfiction. If you have a short story targeted at ages seven or above, look for a suitable magazine.

Another important difference between picture books and short stories is the use of illustrations. Here's author and teacher Christine Kohler again with an explanation.

Christine Kohler on "Is Your Story a Picture Book or a Short Story?"

You are so excited, and for good reason. You have always dreamed of writing a picture book, and now you believe you have come up with the perfect story. You can see it all in your head – adorable colorful illustrations filling every page. Just like the wonderful picture books you have so cherished your entire life.

But then you receive a critique from an expert that says your story is better suited for a magazine than picture book format. Now you are left wondering, *Why? What is the difference between a short story for a magazine and one fitting for a picture book?*

A picture book manuscript should have 10 to 28 pictures implied in the text with a somewhat regular pattern in the words to picture ratio. (Picture books are laid out in multiples of four, and are usually 32 pages, although not all the pages are text. Some of those pages can be front matter, such as the title page, and back matter, such as an author's note. Some pages may have only illustrations.) The illustrations of a picture book should have an integral part in telling the story. In picture books action is essential, and the action turns the page.

"You have to make sure that you have 15 *different* pictures in your story, and they need to be evenly spaced throughout, so the pages keep turning," said Anastasia Suen, author of 135 books and teacher of the online Intensive Picture Book Workshop.

Magazine short stories, however, require fewer illustrations and frequently rely less on them for telling the story.

Patti Gauch, former publisher at Philomel, talks about children's stories being "horizontal" or "vertical," with horizontal stories being better suited for picture books. Those are stories that as you read them you can easily envision the page layout, with the story told as a sequence of illustrated scenes.

Vertical stories are better suited for magazine publishing. These tend to be more internal than external, or might take place entirely in one setting. Some vertical stories are told with only a few distinct scenes tied together by hard-to-illustrate underlying connective tissue such as internalized first-person character thoughts, and these stories work better in magazines.

In picture books, less is more. The purest form of a picture book has no text at all, such as Caldecott winner *The Lion & the Mouse* by Jerry Pinkney. For most books, the illustrations should tell half the story. When writing picture books, the writer needs to trust the illustrator to fill in what is not told in the text.

Picture book language is often lyrical, poetical, even if it doesn't rhyme. Write sparsely, like in poetry. Many editors say they are buying picture books today of only about 100 words or less, no more than about 300 words. More text-heavy picture books are usually for older children, and often historical and/or nonfiction.

On the other hand, short stories written for the magazine markets contain description, narrative, dialogue, and internal monologue. The story must be complete in the reader's mind without illustrations. Although magazines typically do add one or two delightful illustrations to many of the stories, the stories do not depend upon the illustrations for clarification.

If the difference between a short story for a magazine and a picture book is still not clear to you, go the library and declare it "Story Day." Pull out several dozen picture books that have been published within the past five years. (Check the copyright pages in the front of the books.) Now the fun part, read! You can also try typing up the text from some picture books, to see how they look in manuscript format.

Afterwards, go to the magazine section and read stories in children's magazines. After reading, and reading, and reading, it will become clear as to the difference. And it will become clearer when you read your own story as to why it is better suited for a magazine.

If you still want your story to be a picture book instead of a magazine story, you can re-visualize the story and rewrite it for picture book format. But don't pooh-pooh the idea of submitting your short story to a magazine either. Children are delighted and touched deeply by stories, no matter what the format.

Christine Kohler, a graduate of the University of Hawaii, lived in Japan and Guam, the setting for her debut novel *No Surrender Soldier*. She has worked as a reporter, editor and copy editor, media specialist, school teacher, and writing instructor for the Institute of Children's Literature. She has 17 children's books published. Kohler now lives in Texas and is available for teaching writing workshops.

Learn more at www.christinekohlerbooks.com or follow her on Facebook: https://www.facebook.com/ChristineKohlerbooks or Twitter: https://twitter.com/christinekohle1

Chapter 19:
Writing Magazine Nonfiction

Beginning writers often focus on trying to publish picture books or novels. However, many career writers – those who make their living from writing – do at least some nonfiction work for magazines. For example, in the tax year before this writing, I sold over a dozen articles, earning over $3000. Nancy I. Sanders, author of *Yes! You Can Learn How to Write Children's Books, Get Them Published, and Build a Successful Writing Career*, describes the advantages of magazine writing. "There's an unending opportunity to get published and build your writing credentials, especially in the smaller magazines. There are countless topics to write about for each different magazine's focus, so it's easy to find one that matches your personal passion. And finally, there are a significant number of magazines that pay and pay well."

Author, instructor, and free-lance editor Bobi Martin's says, "If I come across a topic that intrigues me, I study *Magazine Markets for Children's Writers* to find magazines that my idea might be a good fit with. Next, I check to see if the age range and word limits of the magazines I've targeted fit with what I had in mind for the article. When I don't have a topic in mind, I study the listings to see what magazine editors are looking for. When I have two or three magazines in mind, I visit their websites for their most current information. This is a great way to generate new topics to write about!"

Checking writer's guidelines is important, because magazines often have strict rules for article lengths and the topics they cover. Some even use theme lists, with each issue covering a specific topic, such as a particular aspect of history or science. Marcia E. Lusted is an Assistant Editor and Staff Writer for e-Pals Publishing, working with the Cobblestone group of children's nonfiction magazines. "My advice would be to really pay attention to what magazines' needs are, particularly if they are themed," she says. "We get so many good queries that just don't fit any of our upcoming themes and we can tell that the writer hasn't bothered to notice that we are themed! The marketing aspect of writing – figuring out what a magazine needs and matching ideas – take time and effort."

One advantage to writing magazine nonfiction is that you can sometimes pitch an idea instead of submitting a completed article. Even if a magazine only accepts finished articles, you can suggest other ideas in your query letter. "When you submit a manuscript or query a magazine with your idea, it also helps to add a list of three to five ideas that might fit well into their particular magazine if your main topic doesn't fit their current needs," Nancy Sanders says. "I've landed more magazine writing assignments over the years by including a short list of other ideas in my query or cover letter for the editor to consider. Giving them the chance to choose another topic if they find merit in your writing helps avoid the constant stream of ambiguous rejections from editors saying, 'Doesn't suit our current needs.'"

Start Small and Focused

While new writers often aim for the best-known magazines, it's easier to break in at smaller specialty or regional publications. *Highlights for Children* may be found in homes, libraries, and doctor's offices across the country, but because it's so well known, the editors receive about 800 manuscript submissions every month. Meanwhile, the lesser-known classroom magazine *Current Health Kids* only receives one or two. Magazines with a narrow and unusual focus may have a hard time getting enough material, so when they find a good writer, they want to build that relationship. You'll find thousands of specialty magazines listed in market guides.

While this book is focusing on writing for children, you might also consider writing for publications aimed at teachers, parents, librarians, or local families. Maybe a city or regional magazine would be interested in an article about a children's museum or a great family vacation spot. Or consider profiling local kids who are doing something interesting. Local or regional magazines can be open to newcomers. "I believe in giving new writers an opportunity to write for our publication," says Susan M. Espinoza, Editor of *enchantment*. The magazine, published by the New Mexico Rural Electric Cooperative Association, is targeted at adults but sometimes profiles local young people. "It spices up the writing, and a new writer may have a new story idea we have never come across before."

Just be prepared to work hard to get that first job. "Research the publication ahead of time," Espinoza suggests. "What is the magazine's target audience and focus? As a new writer, establish a relationship with the editor. Meet the editor's deadlines. Don't hesitate to ask the editor for feedback."

Consider your own interests, talents, and experiences, as Bobi Martin did. "When my daughter became interested in Junior Showmanship, a special class for young people at dog shows, I saw an opportunity to write an article for *Dog World Magazine*. I did my research and sold the article, happy just to have made a sale." Then the editor asked her to cover two kennel club shows a year for the magazine, which led to doing related feature articles and eventually to six years of writing a regular column for Junior Handlers. "Write about topics that matter to you," Martin advises. "You can always research for more information, but if you don't care about your topic, that will show in your writing."

And if you still dream of being featured in a well-known magazine? You can submit work there as well. But looking at less competitive magazines can help you build your skills, get some writing credits, and maybe even earn a few dollars.

Get in and Stay in

A good way to build a magazine career is to cultivate long-term relationships with a few magazines. After you make that first sale, the door is open a little wider. At the Cobblestone magazines, Lusted says, "If someone has written for us just once or twice, they generally follow the same query process as everyone else, although the editor will definitely look at them more favorably because they've already written for us. They might also be more willing to give some feedback on a query or tweak it a little."

As the relationship develops, it typically gets even easier to make a sale. "Their queries might be slightly less detailed, and they won't need to send a writing sample," Lusted says.

Most editors are delighted to find writers who will take on regular assignments. Espinoza says, "You get to know the writing style of the writer, and know what type of stories to assign the writer. A regular writer knows what *enchantment* is about, who the readers are, so he or she knows what types of stories to pitch. Regular writers also understand your deadlines. We build a relationship over time."

That can turn into steady work. At Cobblestone, some writers query for nearly every issue, and the editors may even ask these regulars to fill empty slots. "They know these people write well and will deliver a quality product on time," Lusted says, "and there aren't any unexpected nasty surprises when someone's actual article doesn't live up to their query. I can think of five or six writers for each of our magazines who are published in almost every issue, and some have even ended up doing regular departments. However, to get to this point, a writer has to be willing to write on any topic that the editor gives them."

To build a magazine career, the path is clear: find your passion, explore a niche, target specialty magazines, and develop long-term relationships with editors.

Explore the Magazine Markets:

Magazine Markets for Children's Writers:
Children's Writers and Illustrator's Market:
The SCBWI "Magazine Market Guide" is in *The Book*, included with membership: https://www.scbwi.org/online-resources/the-book/

Get magazine samples at your library, school, or house of worship; requests sample copies from the publisher; or visit publishers' web sites to see if they have online samples.

A list of children's magazines with links to their websites: http://www.monroe.lib.in.us/childrens/kidsmags.html

Analyze magazines for content and style:

Study the cover and slogan: what is the magazine's focus?

What can you learn from the table of contents?
- Are many articles written by one person? Is that person listed in the masthead as staff?
- Are there regular departments? Who writes these?
- This page may include submission guidelines.

Study the content:
- What types of stories/articles does the magazine use? Be as specific as possible, listing fiction genres, nonfiction topics, types of activities, and so forth.
- Does everything relate to one theme?
- What is the breakdown of fiction, nonfiction, activities, and regular departments?
- How long are most pieces?

- How are pieces illustrated? What kind of sidebars do they use, if any? (A sidebar is a short piece of extra information, possibly set off in a box. It may include fun facts, a bulleted list, an example, or other information that relates to the main topic but doesn't quite fit in the main article.)
- Does the magazine use advertising? What kinds of products are advertised? (This can give you insight into reader interests and the magazine's goals.)

Study several stories or articles:
- Are they geared toward girls, boys, or both?
- What age range?
- What can you tell about the magazine's style? Is it wholesome or edgy? Is it focused on health, history, science, religion, or celebrity gossip? Is there a certain tone? As one example, if a magazine uses recipes, are they healthy, or very easy, or fun to look at, etc.

Appropriate ideas:

What kinds of stories or article would your target magazine want? You could start by figuring out what topics the magazine might like, and see if any interest you. Or you could write down a list of your hobbies and interests, and then check which ones might fit that magazine.

When developing an idea, keep the focus narrow. Think "how hummingbirds hover" rather than simply "hummingbirds." Try "the invention of the fork" rather than "a history of utensils." You'll only have a few hundred words, so it's better to go deep into a narrow topic than to skim over a broad topic.

Then Ask:

- Is this idea appropriate for the magazine's readership age? Will they understand and be interested in the topic?
- Can I write this story or article within the magazine's word limits? Do I need to focus it more?
- What is the theme (message) of my story? What will readers take away from my article?
- Why would the reader be interested?

Some types of articles:

Informational
Profile/Interview
Q&A
How-to
Craft/ Recipe
Puzzle
Personal Experience
Self-Help

Nonfiction Article Self-Editing Checklist

Nancy I. Sanders offers this checklist for nonfiction writers. Use it to make sure your article or nonfiction book manuscript is as strong as it can be. Nancy explains:

Kids learn how to self-edit their stories in school. We as writers can, too! Read over your article in multiple sessions to check that it contains the elements nonfiction articles should have. Note "Yes" if you're satisfied. Mark "No" if an item on this list falls short.

Then polish your manuscript until it shines. Don't worry or stress about getting it perfect, though. Submit it when it's the best you know how to write it at this stage of your career.

CONTENT
- I wrote a beginning that introduced the main idea of my topic.
- I wrote a middle that included interesting details, descriptions, and anecdotes
that supported and developed my main idea.
- I wrote an ending that wrapped up the main idea in a satisfying conclusion.

CREATIVE NONFICTION TECHNIQUES
- Every statement, dialogue quote, and detail is 100% true.
- Sensory details were added when appropriate to bring the article to life.
- The Three-Act structure was incorporated to pace the article effectively.
- I remembered to "show, don't tell" by using key anecdotes to replace narrative.

RESEARCH

- The bibliography is formatted correctly.
- All quotes are properly cited with footnotes.
- Each fact is supported by one primary source or three reliable secondary sources.
- I used at least one primary source to authenticate my research.

MECHANICS AND GRAMMAR

- I wrote complete sentences starting with a capital letter and ending with a punctuation mark.
- I used commas, quotation marks, and other punctuation correctly.
- If I wasn't sure about punctuation or grammar, I looked up the rule in a style guide such as *The Chicago Manual of Style* or Jan Venolia's *Write Right!*
- I replaced weak verbs with active verbs, chose succinct words to replace wordy

  phrases, and chose words carefully that helped support my main idea better.

TARGET AUDIENCE

- I read this aloud to my pets, critique buddies, and stray kids to see if it makes sense, flows smoothly, and is interesting enough to keep their attention.
- High-level topics are worded in ways my target age can understand.
- It follows the structure of a published nonfiction article in my target magazine.
- It meets the submission guidelines my target magazine requires.

Nancy I. Sanders is the award-winning and bestselling children's author of over 100 books. For more tips on writing, get Nancy's how-to book for children's writers, *Yes! You Can Learn How to Write Children's Books, Get Them Published, and Build a Successful Writing Career* at http://yesyoucanlearn.wordpress.com

Chapter 20:
Writing Nonfiction Books for Kids

Christine Liu-Perkins shares lessons she learned writing her first book, nonfiction aimed at readers ages 9 to 12.

My debut book, *At Home in Her Tomb: Lady Dai and the Ancient Chinese Treasures of Mawangdui*, took fourteen years from inspiration to publication. I had time to learn a few things along the way.

Choose a Topic Big Enough to Sustain Your Interest

Writing a nonfiction book can take several years. If I'm not sure how long I can stay interested in a topic, I may write an article about it rather than aim for a book. But when I started doing research on the Mawangdui tombs, I discovered they had so many amazing artifacts and revealed so much about life in ancient China – there was more than enough for a book. As I got further in, I could see a large web of connections between the tombs and other topics (e.g., forensics, art, and mourning traditions). Fortunately, my vision kept on growing with each draft I wrote, so I never lost interest.

Do Your Homework

My first proposal used 33 sources, the proposal that got accepted had 61 sources, and the final manuscript had over 400 sources. Collecting all that information was crucial for giving me facts, insights, and high impact details to enrich the book and to ensure accuracy. A friend once asked me, "Do you get tired of doing so much work?"

My answer: there are two sides. I accept that I have to track down lots of sources, read them all, take notes, organize those notes, and let my mind wrestle with the chaos of so much information – that's the time-consuming work part. But I do all that willingly because of the fun part – learning new things, seeing connections, and enjoying the writing because I have lots of wonderful stuff to work with.

Know Why You're Writing the Book

Fourteen years is a long time to keep one's motivation up. Periodically along the way, I journaled about why I was writing this book, what I wanted it to be, who I was writing for, and what I hoped readers would take with them from it. Keeping these in mind helped sustain my faith in the value of pursuing the book.

Be Tenacious

I had plenty of opportunities to practice tenaciousness in every stage of the process. A few examples:

It took eight years and six proposals before the book was acquired.

I traveled to China to see the artifacts and the site of the Mawangdui tombs. My local guide took me to the museum, but three separate times he balked at taking me to the tomb site. "There's nothing to see," he insisted. Having come all the way from the other side of the world, I had to see where Lady Dai had lain hidden for two thousand years. After the third balk, I told him, "Even if it's been built over and there's only a sign marking the spot, I want to see the tomb site." Finally, we went. Two of the tombs had been built over, but the third was open. I felt stunned staring down into the 33-foot deep, cavernous pit – an experience no photo or description could have given me.

A few chapters worked well from the beginning, but others were a struggle. I had to keep trying different approaches, trusting I could figure out how to make the chapters or sections meaningful and compelling.

Think of Nonfiction Writing as Answering Questions

I realized that the book would need questions in search of answers that pulled the reader into the book and all the way through to the end. Questions like, What do the artifacts tell us about the people in the three tombs – their lifestyle, their daily activities, their beliefs and concerns?

This approach helped me sort through information from more than four hundred sources. It helped me decide what to keep in, what to leave out, and what readers would need to know to understand the facts and related issues. Questions also helped me figure out the structure of each chapter individually as an outline of logical flow from one question to its answer to the next, related question.

As I began writing each chapter, I thought about what questions a reader would want answered. For example, in the chapter on Lady Dai's mysterious cadaver, I thought readers would want to know:

- What was the condition of Lady Dai's body when it was found?
- An autopsy was performed on her cadaver. What is an autopsy? What can be learned from an autopsy?
- What did the doctors discover about Lady Dai's body?
- How did she die?
- What is the normal process of decomposition?
- How might bodies avoid decomposition? What processes have been used to preserve bodies?
- How was Lady Dai's body preserved?
- Are there other cadavers like Lady Dai's?

I then wrote the chapter focused on answering those questions in ways that would (hopefully!) capture readers' attention and leave them satisfied at the end – well, at least until the cliffhanger question leading into the next chapter . . ..

Write, Revise, Repeat

First drafts are rarely good enough for professional publication. But in my early years of writing for children when critiques from fellow writers or editors came in, I didn't know how to address the issues they raised. I couldn't see how to change what I had written. Sure, I could make minor tweaks in wording and add or drop sentences here and there. But I was baffled by how to make bigger changes.

Through time and rejections, plus studying others' work and advice, I realized that if I didn't learn to revise, my chances of publishing were slim. Like the odds of hitting a bull's-eye on a first throw – possible but highly unlikely.

A strategy that helps me get beyond seeing only one way to write a chapter, article, or story is to brainstorm multiple openings. For thirty minutes or so, I push myself to keep writing until I've created up to six different ways. Writing multiple openings lets me experiment with the tone, focus, structure, etc. It eliminates the pressure of getting it right the first time. And usually this process clarifies which opening is most promising: the one that makes me want to keep writing (and hopefully, makes the reader want to keep reading).

My developing revision skills served me well on my first book, well enough to earn this comment from my editor regarding the second draft: "I was blown away by the quality of your revision; you did everything I asked for and more, really going above and beyond."

Example:

One chapter in my book, *At Home in her Tomb*, describes a library with texts more than two thousand years old. How could I start the chapter in a way that would draw readers in? Here are several openings I drafted:

1. A library in ancient China would look very different from a modern library. Modern libraries have rectangular volumes standing upright on shelves with titles printed on the edge. Ancient Chinese bookshelves held rolls of bamboo strips or scrolls of silk lying horizontally with titles on tags hanging down from one end.

2. A well-stocked time capsule would contain documents revealing the thoughts and beliefs of people who lived during that period. The Mawangdui tombs provide an amazing array of information to help us understand how people in that time and place viewed the natural world and their lives within it.

3. Judging by the library buried with him, the son [of the Marquis and Lady Dai] was well-educated in the knowledge of his times. Thanks to him, that knowledge passed safely through millennia down to us.

4. Each of the three tombs at Mawangdui contained valuable treasures. The most amazing discovery from the son's tomb was an underground library of silk and bamboo books. These books covered a wide range of topics – medicine, philosophy, history, science, and geography. Scholars were very excited about these books because much of their contents had been lost for centuries when copies were destroyed in fires, wars, and through rotting away.

5. A rectangular lacquer box lay in the east compartment of the son's burial chamber. Its black, undecorated outside gave no hint of the valuables hidden within. When archaeologists lifted the lid, they found numerous folded rectangles of silk, two lengths of silk wrapped around a stick, and two rolls of bamboo and wooden

strips. The silks and strips were covered with writing. What were they?

Question: which opening do you think works best?

When I look back on my years of researching and writing the book, was it worth the marathon wait, the countless hours of work, the roller-coaster of ups and downs? I believe so. It's a wondrous feeling to hold in my hands a book that I poured my heart, mind, and soul into. I appreciate the amazing journey it took to reach this point, and I'm grateful to the many people around the world who helped make the book come to life.

Nonfiction Resources

Thinking Like Your Editor: How to Write Great Serious Nonfiction – and Get It Published, by Susan Rabiner and Alfred Fortunato

Storycraft: The Complete Guide to Writing Narrative Nonfiction, by Jack Hart

The Craft of Research (3rd edition), by Wayne C. Booth, Gregory G. Colomb and Joseph M. Williams

Anatomy of Nonfiction: Writing True Stories for Children, by Margery Facklam and Peggy Thomas

Celebrate Science, a blog by author Melissa Stewart, provides tips for writing nonfiction: http://celebratescience.blogspot.com/

The Nonfiction Detectives blog, with book reviews by two librarians: http://www.nonfictiondetectives.com/

Nonfiction Monday, a weekly roundup of NF book reviews by multiple bloggers: https://nonfictionmonday.wordpress.com/

Nonfiction Picture Book Workshop, an online course taught by Anastasia Suen: http://anastasiasuen.com/nonfiction-picture-book-workshop/

Chapter 21:
Diversity in Children's Literature

We live in a world of many races, cultures, and religions. Children's literature should reflect that diversity, but white, Christian characters and culture dominate. One recent study found that of children's books with human characters, only about 10% featured nonwhite characters. Yet more than 37% of the US population is nonwhite, and that percentage is growing. (In these figures, Hispanic/Latino people and characters are counted as nonwhite.)

Many publishers want books that show diversity, and they hope their offerings will reach a general audience. They want characters from a variety of cultures, and stories where race is not necessarily important to the plot: school stories, fantasy, science fiction, and more, where some characters simply happen to show our world's vast diversity

Alvina Ling, VP and editor-in-chief at Little, Brown Books for Young Readers, says, "There were few depictions of contemporary Asian Americans in the books I read growing up, and I really hungered for them. I also think that it's helpful for children (and adults) to read books that feature characters of many different backgrounds – this helps foster communication and acceptance between different cultural groups."

Writing Across Cultures

Some authors may wonder if they have the "right" to write about other cultures, or fear being accused of appropriating another culture's voice. Yet most editors feel an author's background is a distant second to writing skill. "I'm always looking for authors of color, because we need diverse voices," Ling says. "However, I'm open to books written by authors of any color for multicultural subjects."

Criticism does happen. Jodi Lea Stewart says, "Growing up on a ranch in the Arizona White Mountains wedged between two major Native American tribes contributed greatly to my decision to write the *Silki, the Girl of Many Scarves* trilogy. The novels feature a Navajo protagonist living in a contemporary Navajo Nation. When I first considered the idea of writing outside my own culture, I encountered excitement from many Navajos, skepticism from a few, and outright antagonism from others. The objections raised seemed to center on the fact that I wasn't Diné (Navajo), so how could I possibly understand their ways? 'Why don't you write in your own backyard?' some asked me. Actually, I was doing just that. I had been one of only seven Caucasian children at the school I attended in Concho, Arizona. My classmates were Hispanic, Apache, or Navajo. We were friends. Learning companions. Playground buddies. My goal was to honor them by bringing a positive public light into their cultures. Some people 'got that' and others turned away."

Stewart went forward with her project. She says, "To write about a culture very different from one's own takes raw courage, as well as a commitment to the deepest level of research to find the authentic voice and cadence that ultimately brings light and understanding to that group of people. What one may discover in this expedition is an almost effervescent reality that people of all cultures truly share more similarities than diversities. That alone will make the journey extraordinary."

Cynthia Leitich Smith writes fantasies for teens. *Eternal* features a Chinese-Scottish American protagonist and *Tantalize: Kieren's Story* has an Irish-Mexican American protagonist. "Folks have speculated that because I'm a biracial person, married to a biracial person, I'm especially comfortable with it," she notes. "But the reality is that you simply can't reflect this world, either literally or in fantasy, without incorporating a diversity of people and cultures."

People who draw on their own experiences in a diverse world can create multicultural stories that explore deeper questions of how cultures interact. Of her *Young Inventors Guild* series, Eden Unger Bowditch says, "The secret history of this story goes back centuries and reaches across continents. The characters come from different parts of the world and find that, against their differences and against the dangers they face together, they become something of a family. As the mystery unfolds, they come to understand how the brotherhood of science is more than a common language but the very link that connects them."

She adds, "Personally, living as an expat [in her case, an American in Egypt] has brought so many diverse and compelling people into my life. Being expats, we are all drawn together. In this sense, the children of the *Young Inventors Guild* are expats, as it is a strange world in which they find themselves. It creates a unique bond among them that gives them strength to uncover the truth."

Justina Chen's characters include a rich Chinese-American girl in *Girl Overboard* and a blonde, white girl with a port-wine birthmark in *North of Beautiful*. She says, "While I certainly have written about multicultural issues, I hesitate to be seen as a multicultural author. I think it's important that authors of color be given the same as license others to write about dragons and vampires and white girls — and whatever other stories move them."

Including Diversity of Love and Gender

Race, culture, and religion are only a small part of diversity. Here's writer and blogger Lee Wind to share thoughts on another aspect:

Whether you're writing picture books to be read to the littlest kids or novels for teens to read themselves, it's important to remember that not all boys grow up to fall in love with girls — some boys will grow up to fall in love with other boys! Same for girls. Same for their parents. And teachers. And coaches.

And while 10% or so of actual young people will grow up to be gay, lesbian, or bisexual (or even asexual), out of the total of about 5,000 traditionally published books each year for kids and teens, less than 100 have significant gay, lesbian, or bisexual characters. And while those numbers are rising, there's still a long way to go.

It's easy to get caught up in thinking that including sexual orientation means we have to write about sex, but even in the classic children's stories, consider how many *happily ever afters* reinforce the idea that every girl wants and 'should' end up with a prince.

Having said that, every character (Lesbian, Gay, Bisexual, Asexual, *and* Heterosexual) needs to be three-dimensional and even flawed in some way. Be aware of stereotypes and avoid the clichés. Just like when writing outside our own cultural background, we need to do our homework, and run it by someone who is a member of that community to make sure we're doing our character justice.

Gender variety and gender non-conformity is another area where representation in children's and teen literature is scant, with still only a handful of books for young people published each year.

No matter what we're writing, we need to be aware that we may be reinforcing the idea that there are only two kinds of people: boys and girls. This is problematic because that binary isn't accurate. There are many people who identify as gender fluid, others as gender queer, others as intersex, and still others as transgender*. (The asterisk is there to note and include the seemingly ever-expanding ways to self-identify.)

And when writing our characters (even those that solidly identify as gender conforming 'boys' and 'girls') we should consider whether or not we are reinforcing a 1950s mentality of what is 'okay' or appropriate for what gender. Are all our adults in positions of authority men? Who are the wage-earners in our characters' families? Who are the heroes/heroines? The villains? Who wears pink? Who doesn't? How do characters react to gender non-conformity? Every choice we make shapes the world of our story, and reflects to readers the possibilities in their own lives.

If LGBTQAI+ (the plus is like the asterisk, to include anyone that doesn't feel their identity is included in the acronym standing for Lesbian, Gay, Bisexual, Transgender, Queer, Questioning, Asexual and Intersex) – if LGBTQAI+ kids today don't see their reflection in books, how can they grow up to believe they have a place in our real world? And for the heterosexual and gender-conforming kids, the message is doubly important. If our stories don't include diversity of love and gender, how will they treat that diversity when they encounter it in their lives? What kind of world do we want our writing to help create?

Sometimes writers shy away from including LGBTQAI+ diversity due to fear that it might make it harder to get that first book published, harder to make their dream come true. On the contrary, many agents and editors have shared that including these diverse characters can make a submitted work stand out for them! It still needs to be a compelling story told from the heart with finesse, but in today's publishing landscape, including diversity of love and diversity of gender can actually help you get published.

Lee Wind., M.Ed. is a blogger, writer and speaker. His award-winning blog for LGBTQ teens and their allies, "I'm Here. I'm Queer. What the Hell Do I Read?" (at http://www.leewind.org/) has had over 1.4 million visits! He is also the official blogger for SCBWI, The Society of Children's Book Writers and Illustrators (at http://scbwi.blogspot.com/.)

Physical and Mental Conditions

Diversity involves many aspects of biology and culture. People of all ages have a variety of physical and mental abilities/illnesses. One young reader could be going through cancer treatment. Another may be blind or deaf. One might be on the autism spectrum or have just received a diagnosis of ADHD. Some children need to use wheelchairs. Some suffer from depression or an anxiety disorder.

Other young readers have family members with special needs, physical challenges, or mental illnesses. These kids may have responsibilities the average young person doesn't have because of unusual family demands. Finally, some children suffer from physical, mental, or sexual abuse, which can also contribute to mental health conditions such as Post-Traumatic Stress Disorder (PTSD). Kids whose lives have not been affected in any of these ways still benefit from knowing about these situations. It helps them understand and empathize with their classmates, and it helps prepare them for challenges they could face in the future.

Jim Tritten, a writer and a volunteer for the National Alliance on Mental Illness, says, "You can't just pretend that all kids grow up in a normal, functional household. If a kid is having an issue at home, and he's reading a book dealing with that issue, the subtle message should be, number one, you're not alone, and number two, you need to tell someone about it." He's worked with adults who are still processing childhood traumas, because they were not addressed when they happened. "In the kids' case, they won't seek help because they're afraid, they're ashamed." Books can offer comfort and even encourage young people to seek help.

Suzanne Morgan Williams says, "My novel, *Bull Rider,* is the story of how Cam O'Mara helps himself and his older brother, Ben, when Ben returns from Iraq with a severe TBI [traumatic brain injury], having lost an arm, and initially unable to walk and talk. At first I minimized Ben's injuries because I was uncomfortable with them myself. But as I wrote his character, I realized that he was still there, still the man he'd been – just changed. Good stories are about change and change comes to everyone. It doesn't matter if a character is mentally or physically challenged, they can change.

"Disabled people can be interesting characters," she adds. "Just don't depend on your assumptions or even on one friend for your information. Talk to experts, talk to families. Be sure you aren't stereotyping the character because above all else – any other injury, happenstance of birth, personality trait – your character is a *person*. Make your subject as complex, emotional (perhaps in their own way), silly, angry – whatever – as anyone else. A mentally or physically challenged person can hold his own in your manuscript if you research, avoid stereotypes, and let their personalities shine.

Stacie Ramey is the author of *The Sister Pact*, which deals with the effects of depression. She says, "Children with disabilities should be included in books for teens because they are part of the community. They are someone's brother, friend, sister. They have the same exact stories to tell. It's up to us to tell them in a way that makes them feel real and relatable. But when writing children with disabilities, it's important to remember that they want the same things as their non-disabled friends do. They want to connect. They want to be accepted. They want to feel safe. They want to be the hero. They want to do important things. They want to win. So if you're going to put children with disabilities in your manuscripts, make them real."

Putting It All Together

Finally, it's worth noting that books can include characters from more than one category of diversity. Christine Kohler's novel *No Surrender Soldier* is set on Guam during the Vietnam war era. The characters are nearly all non-Caucasian, mainly Chamorros – indigenous Pacific Islanders in the Mariannas – or Japanese, or mixed Chamorro and Japanese. The main character's grandfather has a disease similar to dementia. Two other characters have PTSD. That's a lot going on in one book, but it reflects the complexity of real life. Strong storytelling means the novel is still accessible to the average teenager. According to the review journal *Booklist*, "This debut transports readers to an exotic place in a troubled time and reveals that being a teenager in Guam is not so different from being a teen elsewhere in the world." By finding commonalities among differences, a writer can introduce young readers to different experiences and viewpoints.

Kohler, who lived and worked in Japan and Guam before writing *No Surrender Soldier*, says, "Experience and research can create authenticity in writing about people of other ethnicities, cultures, religions, genders, and physical conditions. Stereotyping comes from lack of research or experience. The less personal experience the writer has with a character different in any way from the writer, and setting and culture foreign to what the writer has experienced, calls for deeper research.

"Don't restrict your research to internet and books, Kohler adds. "The best characters spring from the writer's keen observations of people in their natural environment. Go on a field trip. Researching food can be yummy. Attending services in a mosque, temple, synagogue, or church can be mind-broadening and inspirational. Volunteering at hospitals and homeless shelters can be humbling and soul-enriching. Be sensitive to those you are representing in your characters. Reflecting diversity is more than differences one sees on the outside in customs or behaviors. It is often a completely different mindset."

If you are going to write diverse characters, perhaps you'll draw on your own experiences. Remember to try to capture the child or teen's view, rather than writing from an adult outside viewpoint, either looking back at your childhood or analyzing your own children.

If you don't have personal experience, devote time to research and interviews, and perhaps have an expert check over your manuscript. Justina Chen says, "Make sure you have represented the character and culture correctly. Check not just the facts, but the overall feel of the characters with a trusted and honest reader – are the mannerisms and colloquialisms accurate and authentic? Or have you unintentionally used a stereotype?" On the other hand, simply giving a character a different skin color for the sake of diversifying your cast isn't true diversity. The characters have to ring true.

Laurie Thompson is the author of *Emmanuel's Dream*, illustrated by Sean Qualls, an inspirational picture book biography. It tells the true story of a young man with only one leg who bicycled across Ghana. Thompson says, "One of the hardest things about writing *Emmanuel's Dream* was trusting myself to write what I didn't know. I had a lot of doubts about whether a white American woman with no disabilities could or even should tell this story. I realized eventually that I just couldn't let go of it, so I just had to jump in and work extra hard to make it authentic. I spent eight years researching, interviewing (including Emmanuel himself), soliciting feedback, and revising. It paid off!"

Even if you do have personal experience, you still might want to do additional research. There is no single experience with race, culture, gender identity, physical ability, or mental illness. Researching a condition or interviewing people with a certain background can help you create an accurate, well-rounded portrayal.

No Limits

So what does all this talk about diversity mean to you? You don't need to pack your stories full of diverse characters if you don't choose to. However, strong stories today help reflect our diverse world, so consider whether some diversity would be realistic and appealing. And if you are called to write a certain kind of character, know that it is fine to do so. Nothing is automatically "off-limits" in children's literature. The story has to be appropriate for the audience age, and it should be a great story, but within those parameters, anything and everything can work.

Topics can be addressed in different ways, depending on the audience age. For example, *Oskar and Klaus: The Search for Bigfoot* was inspired by two real-life cats, one blind, the other a scarred former stray. Blind Klaus uses his other senses to find the way on their adventure. Books like this, and like Laurie Thompson's *Emmanuel's Dream*, inspire young children as they see characters overcoming adversity to have adventures.

Books for older readers can delve into more challenging subjects. *Silent to the Bone*, by E. L. Konigsburg, is a mystery where the main character tries to find out the truth about his best friend, who is accused of abusing his baby sister and sent to a Juvenile Behavioral Center, where he can't or won't speak. Although the book deals with difficult issues, it's shown through the best friend's view as he investigates the story. This slight distance from the trauma, and the exciting mystery plot, make the novel accessible to the average middle grade reader.

Other novels feature main characters facing challenges in their own lives. *Reign Rain*, by Ann M. Martin, has an autistic heroine. *All the Answers*, by Kate Messner, has a protagonist with anxiety and a magic pencil. In *Fish in a Tree*, by Lynda Mullaly Hunt, a girl tries to hide her dyslexia. *May B.*, by Caroline Starr Rose, has another young heroine with dyslexia, this one abandoned on the Kansas prairie in the 1870s. Jennifer Bohnhoff's historical novel, *The Bent Reed: A Novel about Gettysburg*, has a heroine in a body cast for scoliosis. Middle grade novels such as these share insight into these conditions through appealing characters and stories of mystery, magic, or adventure, in the past, present or future.

In young adult novels, anything goes. Corey Ann Haydu's *OCD Love Story* is a romance about two teenagers struggling with different types of obsessive compulsive disorder. *Rage*, by Jackie Morse Kessler, is a fantasy with a heroine who suffers from depression and anxiety, which she relieves by cutting. *Hunger*, also by Morse Kessler, features an anorexic girl who is called to be Famine, one of the four Riders of the Apocalypse. *Identical*, a novel in verse by Ellen Hopkins, features twin sisters. One is being sexually abused by their father, while the other tries to dull her pain with alcohol, drugs, and sex. While many adults are shocked at how dark some of these books are, they can be wildly popular and can literally save lives. Hopkins's books are bestsellers, and she gets incredible fan mail from teens thanking her for helping them deal with issues in their own lives, or the lives of friends and relatives.

Stories can be dark, but they can also be humorous and optimistic. *Okay for Now*, by Gary Schmidt, a book about a boy with an abusive father, is described as "equal parts comedy and tragedy." Several recent winners of the Sid Fleischman Humor Award tackle realistic issues. *Openly Straight*, by Bill Konigsberg (2014 Winter), features a gay teen deciding whether or not he wants to stay "out" in his new school. *Food, Girls, and Other Things I Can't Have*, by Allen Zadoff (2010 winner), has a hero who is overweight and bullied. In *Milo: Sticky Notes and Brain Freeze*, by Alan Silberberg (2011 winner), a 12-year-old boy is dealing with the death of his mother.

Selling Diversity

Short multicultural nonfiction can find a home in magazines that explore world history or culture. Each issue of *FACES*, for ages 9 to 14, covers a specific country or topic, such as "Family Life Around the World." Personal experience with the culture helps, but the most important thing is writing a kid-friendly article.

The folktale market is weak, but some publishers still produce traditional, retold, or new folktales. Unusual cultures can have special appeal. Teri Sloat wrote and illustrated several Alaskan folktales or contemporary Alaskan stories, including *Berry Magic*, with Betty Huffmon. Translating Yup'ik stories meant going "from literal to literary," she says. "I look for good stories where the story is more important than the backdrop of culture."

When retelling traditional stories, it's important to follow copyright rules. Even if the story is hundreds of years old, the specific way it's told in a recent book is under copyright. Sloat carefully differentiates between retold tales and her original work. "I check the internet and Sourcebook to see if that story, or fragments of it, have been told or collected elsewhere. In other words, what is my telling adding to the book world?"

Books that feature different cultures, especially historical fiction and nonfiction, can benefit if they work well in the classroom. My Mayan novel, *The Well of Sacrifice*, has stayed in print since 1999 because many schools use it when they study the Maya. To target the school market, seek out underrepresented cultures with the appropriate grade level curriculum tie-in, and write a dramatic story.

(The National History Education Clearing House has a database of state social studies and history standards, searchable by state and grade. Find it at: http://teachinghistory.org/teaching-materials/state-standards.)

The demand for diversity does not mean that it is easy to sell a book with a multicultural cast. The story still needs to be excellent, with broad appeal. Stories should attract those of the same background as the characters, but they need to draw a general audience as well. To do that, Kohler says, "Write from the depth of emotion – from love to suffering – that we share in humanity."

Caroline Starr Rose says of *May B.*, "I've come to the conclusion I am qualified to tell May's story because it is one of identity and self-worth — something all of us must face at some point, something that becomes very real to young people as they become aware of their place in this world."

The more diversity our short stories, novels, and nonfiction show, the better we'll reflect real life – and help young people develop compassion and understanding.

Resources for Diversity:

The Children's Book Council CBC Diversity shares news encouraging diversity of race, gender, geographical region, sexual orientation, and class: http://www.cbcdiversity.com/

Cynthia Leitich Smith's Exploring Diversity page has links to book lists about many religions and races, and relevant interviews: http://www.cynthialeitichsmith.com/lit_resources/diversity/multicultural/communities.html

Multiculturalism Rocks! is a blog celebrating multiculturalism in children's literature, with many useful links: http://nathaliemvondo.wordpress.com/

We Need Diverse Books promotes changes in the publishing industry to produce literature that reflects all young people: http://weneeddiversebooks.org/

Disability in Kidlit examines the portrayal of disability in MG and YA literature: http://disabilityinkidlit.com/

Author Lee Wind's blog lists books with gay teen characters or themes, interviews with agents seeking diverse stories, videos on gender identity, and more: http://www.leewind.org/

41 Transgender-friendly Books for Young Kids: http://bitchmagazine.org/post/41-transgender-friendly-books-for-young-kids

SCBWI has grants to promote diversity in children's books: http://www.scbwi.org/awards/grants/grants-to-promote-diversity-in-childrens-books/

Chapter 22:
Resources for Writing for Children

I'm on a listserv of writing teachers, and the question came up of the value of MFA programs. Though none of us are questioning that people get a good education – and often great networking with publishing professionals – these programs can be expensive. As in $36,000 plus travel expenses for one of the best-known low residency children's book writing MFA programs.

Obviously, that's not realistic for everyone, especially if you don't want to go into debt for your education. So what if you feel like you need a better education – or the contacts that come with a respected MFA program?

On the list, we discussed other options. Kristi Holl, author of books for children and books about writing (see below) said she interviewed MFA grads about what their program involved and how they learned the most. The three main components:

- Reading an extensive list of current and classic children's books

- Studying craft books

- Writing and being critiqued

How about doing that on your own? You can find many lists of "best" books. . The American Library Association has many annual awards, including the Newbery (for middle grade books), Caldecott (for picture books), and Prinz (for young adult books). The International Literacy Association has the Children's Choice Reading List. The Society of Children's Book Writers and Illustrators has the Golden Kite Award and the Crystal Kite Award, which is based on a vote by peers. Visit your local bookstore or library, pick up a stack of books, read, and analyze – perhaps with a copy of *Reading like a Writer* or this online guide to "How to Read like a Writer."

There's an enormous amount you could learn about writing in general, writing for children in particular, and the publishing business. Wherever you are in your writing or publishing journey, you'll find books, websites, blogs, and classes that can help. The following is a small sample of what's available, including some of my favorite resources. Additional resources have been provided at the ends of most chapters in this book, where relevant to the chapter topic. See Chapter 15 for advice on joining or starting a critique group.

As Kristi commented, "While this isn't the same as getting an MFA, you CAN study and practice and do a reading list and get a critique group and create your own home-study pseudo-MFA program—and have no debt when you're finished."

The **Society of Children's Book Writers and Illustrators** provides publications on the craft and business of writing and illustrating for young people. SCBWI also publishes a quarterly newsletter and monthly email newsletter. Awards and grants are available for published works and works in progress. SCBWI members can join discussion boards covering a wide variety of craft and business topics. Many states and countries have local branches with regular activities, including conferences and/or retreats: www.scbwi.org.

Print/Ebook Resources:

The Idiot's Guide to Children's Book Publishing, by Harold Underdown, is an excellent overview of the industry. It explains everything from the different genres, to how to find a publisher, all the way through marketing your published book.

Writing Children's Books For Dummies, by Lisa Rojany Buccieri and Peter Economy, is another overview, from getting organized to marketing your published book. (Note: be sure to get the most recent version. A lot has changed since 2005.)

Yes! You Can Learn How to Write Children's Books, Get Them Published, and Build a Successful Writing Career, by Nancy I. Sanders, offers advice on setting goals, managing your time, writing successful queries, and more. She provides great info on building a career as a writer.

The Business of Writing for Children, by Aaron Shepard, cover some of the nuts and bolts of writing. This short book then focuses on the publishing process, from manuscript formatting to contracts to promotion.

Writing Irresistible Kidlit, by Mary Kole, focuses on middle grade and young adult novels.

Yes! You Can Learn How to Write Beginning Readers and Chapter Books, by Nancy I. Sanders, focuses on books for kids learning to read.

Writing Young Adult Fiction For Dummies, by Deborah Halverson, focuses on writing for teenagers.

Anatomy of Nonfiction, by Margery Facklam and Peggy Thomas, delves deeper into the nonfiction market.

Advanced Plotting, by Chris Eboch, provides a tool for analyzing your plot, along with articles on making your work stronger.

Second Sight, by Scholastic editor Cheryl Klein, offers insight into how an editor works, with lots of great craft advice.

Writing It Right! How Successful Children's Authors Revise and Sell Their Stories, by Sandy Asher, studies 21 manuscripts (picture books, magazine stories, novels, and more) from early drafts to revisions. Great insight into the editing process.

Self-Editing for Fiction Writers, by Renni Browne and Dave King, is highly recommended for advice and exercises on improving your style.

Author and writing teacher Kristi Holl offers titles such as *Boundaries for Writers; Writer's First Aid: Getting Organized, Getting Inspired, and Sticking to It; 50 Tension Techniques: Hold a Reader's Attention from Beginning to End;* and *Writing Mysteries for Young People*: http://www.kristiholl.com/writing.php

You'll find many more books about writing in general, writing for kids, or the business side of publishing. See what your library has or browse online for more options.

Web Resources:

Children's author Rachelle Burk's extensive list of Resources for Writers includes writing advice, publisher listings, and information on poetry, nonfiction, query letters, self-publishing, promotion and more: http://resourcesforchildrenswriters.com/

Children's magazines with links to websites:
http://www.monroe.lib.in.us/childrens/kidsmags.html

Harold Underdown's FAQs about the industry:
http://www.underdown.org/basic-articles.htm

Editor Cheryl Klein and writer/director James Monohan's Narrative Breakdown podcast series discusses storytelling techniques: https://itunes.apple.com/us/podcast/narrative-breakdown-podcast/id430791642

Author Janice Hardy has a fantastic blog of craft tips, Fiction University: http://blog.janicehardy.com/

Agent Mary Kole blogs about the craft of writing for children: KidLit.com

Adventures in YA Publishing is a group blog by young adult writers: http://www.adventuresinyapublishing.com/

Project Mayhem is a group blog by middle grade writers:
http://project-middle-grade-mayhem.blogspot.com/

The Cynsations blog by author Cynthia Leitich Smith provides news and lots of links on all aspects of children's literature, especially multicultural books:
http://cynthialeitichsmith.blogspot.com/.

Chris Eboch's blog offers posts on the craft of writing:
http://chriseboch.blogspot.com

At Writing According to Humphrey and Friends, author Nancy Sanders shares information on writing topics such as developing characters and setting. Be sure to check out the "Writer's Notebook Worksheet" page, with a list of worksheets for critiquing manuscripts, getting organized, identifying topics appropriate to different age groups, and much more:
https://writingaccordingtohumphrey.wordpress.com/

Many of these blogs have links to more blogs and other writing sites.

In Conclusion ....

A point I've tried to make in this book is that writing and publishing are different. They are related sometimes, but they are not the same thing. Writing is a craft, while publishing is a business.

Writing can be personal, for yourself or to share with family and friends. It can be a way to capture your thoughts, feelings, and memories. A way to express yourself and share your vision of the world. A way to expand your creativity and simply have fun.

Publishing involves business terms such as market trends, copyright, and royalty statements. Learning about publishing is interesting and even fun for some people, while others find it intimidating and discouraging. In my opinion, it's best not to worry about the publishing business until you have plenty of experience with the craft of writing. Develop your skills and enjoy yourself. Focusing on the process, rather than the end result, may relieve some of the stress that inevitably comes with submitting your work or releasing it into the world.

But ultimately, while writing versus publishing may be craft versus business, they have one important connection: the reader. What will cause young readers to fall in love with the story, to want to read it over and over, to talk about it with friends? If you bring your skills and passion to creating the story, you have a better chance of attracting young readers. That's where craft and business combine. Young readers are a wonderful audience, and books, stories and articles can have a lasting impact on them.

If you do have dreams of publication – and maybe even financial success, fame, and awards – I wish you success. You may not reach your goals as soon as you'd like (few of us do). But if it turns out that some of your beloved stories are merely "practice" stories while you learn your craft, don't fret. Nothing is truly wasted, not a sentence or page that got thrown away, not a minute of your time spent studying or creating. The work leads to a better understanding of writing for children. It leads to better stories. Ultimately, it may lead to publication or however you define success.

I hope this book will lead you farther down the path on your writing journey, wherever that path may take you.

About the Author

Chris Eboch writes fiction and nonfiction for all ages, with 30+ traditionally published books for children. Chris is an Regional Advisor Emerita for SCBWI and has given popular writing workshops around the world.

Sign up for information on her workshop and webinars, and occasional special offers for critiques: http://eepurl.com/040_j

Learn more about Chris's books and read excerpts at www.chriseboch.com. Sign up for her author newsletter at http://eepurl.com/8MQmX

Chris also writes novels of suspense and romance for adults under the name Kris Bock.

Kris Bock novels involve outdoor adventures and Southwestern landscapes. *The Mad Monk's Treasure* follows the hunt for a long-lost treasure in the New Mexico desert. In *The Dead Man's Treasure*, estranged relatives compete to reach a buried treasure by following a series of complex clues. In *Counterfeits*, stolen Rembrandt paintings bring danger to a small New Mexico town. *Whispers in the Dark* features archaeology and intrigue among ancient Southwest ruins. *What We Found* is a mystery with romantic elements about a young woman who finds a murder victim in the woods.

Learn more at www.krisbock.com.

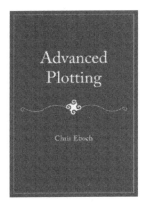

Advanced Plotting is designed for the intermediate and advanced writer. Read the book straight through, study the index to find help with your current problem, or dip in and out randomly – however you use this book, you'll find fascinating insights and detailed tips to help you build a stronger plot and become a better writer.

"This really is helping me a lot. It's written beautifully and to-the-point. The essays really help you zero in on your own problems in your manuscript. The Plot Outline Exercise is a great tool!"

"I just read and dissected your well written book: Advanced Plotting. It's now highlighted in bright orange and littered with many of those little 3M sticky labels. GOOD JOB."

Middle Grade Fiction by Chris

Shy and timid Anise determines to find the Genie Shakayak and claim the Gift of Sweet Speech. But the way is barred by a series of challenges, both ordinary and magical. How will Anise get past a vicious she-ghoul, a sorceress who turns people to stone, and mysterious sea monsters, when she can't even speak in front of strangers?

The Genie's Gift is a lighthearted action novel set in the fifteenth-century Middle East, drawing on the mythology of *The Arabian Nights*.

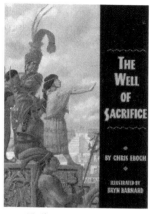

In *The Well of Sacrifice*, a Mayan girl in ninth-century Guatemala rebels against the High Priest who sacrifices anyone challenging his power.

"[An] engrossing first novel.... The novel shines not only for a faithful recreation of an unfamiliar, ancient world, but also for the introduction of a brave, likable and determined heroine." – *Kirkus Reviews*

"The adventures of this tenacious heroine are suspenseful and entertaining, providing readers with an exciting story and a realistic feel for everyday life in and ceremonial practices of the ancient Mayan culture. Well-researched historical fiction and a good read." – *School Library Journal*

"Watching this unorthodox 12-year-old girl outwit a high priest, escape jail, rescue her sister and more makes for a fast-paced read. An author's note describes the historical context for the tale." – *Publishers Weekly*

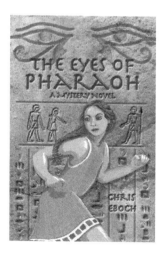

The Eyes of Pharaoh: 1177 BC. When Reya claims that Egypt is in danger from foreign nomads, Seshta and Horus don't believe anyone could challenge Egypt.

Then Reya disappears. To save their friend, Seshta and Horus spy on merchants, soldiers, and royalty, and start to suspect even The Eyes of Pharaoh, the powerful head of the secret police. Will Seshta and Horus escape the traps set for them, rescue Reya, and stop the plot against Egypt in time?

John doesn't believe in ghosts. Not even if his mother does, and married a man who researches ghost sightings for his own TV show. Not even when they travel with the show, and visit "haunted" places.

But his younger sister Tania claims she can see the ghosts. Deciding to believe her is just the first challenge. Softhearted Tania wants to help the ghosts. First the siblings have to find out what happened to keep each ghost trapped in this world. Then they have to help the ghosts move on—sometimes by letting them take over Tania's body. All this while dealing with their overprotective mother, a stepfather who'd want to exploit Tania's gift, and a production assistant who's totally hot but impossible to impress.

Life gets interesting when your sister sees ghosts. And the TV show's shooting season is just beginning....

Books in the *Haunted* series:

The Ghost on the Stairs is set at a Colorado hotel haunted by a ghost bride from the 1880s who is waiting for her missing husband to return.

The Riverboat Phantom features a steamboat pilot still trying to prevent a long-ago disaster.

In *The Knight in the Shadows*—winner of the 2010 New Mexico Book Awards in the category Juvenile Book—a Renaissance French squire protects a sword on display at a New York City museum.

During *The Ghost Miner's Treasure*, Jon and Tania help a dead man find his lost gold mine—but they're not the only ones looking for it.

Danger in the Wilderness....

While hiking in the mountains, Jesse meets a strange trio. He befriends Maria, but he's suspicious of the men with her. Still, charmed by Maria, Jesse promises not to tell anyone that he met them. But his new friends have deadly secrets, and Jesse uncovers them. It will take all his wilderness skills, and all his courage, to survive.

Readers who enjoyed Gary Paulsen's *Hatchet* will love *Bandits Peak*. This heart-pounding adventure tale is full of danger and excitement.

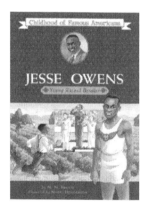

Jesse Owens: Young Record Breaker and *Milton Hershey: Young Chocolatier* are heartwarming fictionalized biographies in Simon & Schuster's Childhood of Famous Americans series, written under the name M.M. Eboch.

Be inspired by the struggles these amazing people had to overcome to reach success.

36144380R00092

Printed in Great Britain
by Amazon